Badger State Showmen

A History of Wisconsin's Circus Heritage

by Fred Dahlinger, Jr. and Stuart Thayer

A publication of
Circus World Museum

Grote Publishing
Madison, Wisconsin

A publication of   Circus World Museum is owned by the
Circus World Museum   State Historical Society of Wisconsin
426 Water Street   Madison, WI
Baraboo, WI 53913-2597
(608) 356-8341

Designed and published by
Grote Publishing
634 West Main Street, Suite 207
Madison, WI 53703-2634
(608) 257-4640

Printed in the U.S.A.

Library of Congress Cataloging-in-Publication Data
Dahlinger, Fred, 1951—
        Badger State Showmen: A History of Wisconsin's Circus Heritage /
                Fred Dahlinger, Jr. & Stuart Thayer.
                        p.   cm.
        Includes bibliographical references (p.) and index.
        ISBN 0-9663436-1-1 (hardcover)
        1. Circus owners—Wisconsin—Biography.   I. Thayer. Stuart.
        2. Circus performers—Wisconsin—Biography.   II. Title.
        3. Circus—Wisconsin—History.
        GV1811.A1D35 1998
        791.3'092—dc21   98-45989
        [b]   CIP

This project has been funded in part by the Wisconsin Sesquicentennial Commission, with funds from the State of Wisconsin and individual and corporate contributors. We'd like to express our appreciation for the generosity of these corporations and recognize their contributions.

FOUNDER

ANR Pipeline Company
Alliant-Wisconsin Power & Light Foundation
Blue Cross/Blue Shield United Wisconsin
Color Ink, Inc.
DEC International, Inc.
Fortis Insurance Company
General Casualty Companies
Home Savings
John Deere Horicon Works
Johnson Controls
Kikkoman Foods, Inc.
Kohler Co.
Marcus Theatres Corporation
Michael, Best & Friedrich
Midwest Express Airlines
Nicolet Minerals Company
Northwestern Mutual Life Foundation
Promega Corporation
Robert W. Baird & Co., Inc.
Snap-on Incorporated
Weyerhaeuser
Wisconsin Central Ltd.
Wisconsin Department of Tourism
Wisconsin Public Service Foundation
Wisconsin State Cranberry Growers Association

TRAILBLAZER

AT&T
SC Johnson Wax
The Credit Unions of Wisconsin

VOYAGEUR

Firstar Corporation
Harley-Davidson, Inc.
Marshall & Ilsley Corporation
Milwaukee Journal Sentinel
Outdoor Advertising Association
Philip Morris Companies:
    Miller Brewing Company
    Kraft Foods/Oscar Mayer Foods Corp.
    Philip Morris USA
W.H. Brady Co.
Weber-Stephen Products Co.
Wisconsin Manufacturers & Commerce

BADGER

3M
Aid Association for Lutherans
Allen-Edmonds Shoe Corp.
A.O. Smith Corporation
Badger Mining Corporation
Briggs & Stratton Corporation
Case Corporation
Consolidated Papers, Inc.
Dairyland Power Cooperative
Eller Media Company
Fort James Corporation
Fraser Papers
Fred Usinger Inc.
Green Bay Packaging, Inc.
International Paper
Jockey International, Inc.
Jorgensen Conveyors, Inc.
Kimberly-Clark Corporation
Mann Bros., Inc.
Marathon Communications
Marcus Corporation
Marshfield Clinic
Milwaukee Brewers
Modine Manufacturing Company
National Business Furniture, Inc.
Oscar J. Boldt Construction Co.
Pizza Pit, Ltd.
Rockwell Automation/Allen-Bradley
Rust Environment & Infrastructure
Schneider National
ShopKo
Stevens Point Brewery
The Edgewater
Twin Disc, Incorporated
United States Cellular
Virchow, Krause & Company, LLP
Walters Buildings
Wausau and Mosinee Papers Corporation Foundation
Wisconsin Bakers Association Inc.
Wisconsin Counties Association
Wisconsin Physicians Service Insurance Corporation

Additional support provided by Bill Griffith, Spring Green, Wisconsin.

CONTENTS

PREFACE

To the farmers and villagers of nineteenth-century Wisconsin, circus day was a festival of marvels, just as the press agents advertised it to be. The posting of a circus bill in the local inn or livery stable began a period of expectation that affected young and old alike. The promise of exotic sights, of a caravan coming from afar, of fine horses and accomplished athletes, set pulses tingling. Children were the most excited, but their elders also spent at least a few minutes contemplating the wonders spelled out and illustrated on the "flaming bills."

In an age when hard work was the lot of all and pleasures were few and far between, the bustle of circus day in a small town was a welcome treat. Even one who heeded the preacher's warning and did not attend the performance could appreciate the hubbub that accompanied the event.

Early in the morning teams began arriving in town, bringing farm families who lived ten to fifteen miles away. Some drove all night to reach the place. The streets were crowded, stores were soon stripped of bologna and cheese and bread, and taverns became filled with those who could not contemplate a sober holiday.

A street parade, no matter how small it might be, was the center of all attention, and it was followed to the circus lot, where the canvas tent had risen from a bare field that very morning.

The circusgoers dressed as if for church: girls in their lace and bonnets, young men in their best coats and hats. There was much visiting and picnicking on the grounds. Booths were set up where one could buy gingerbread, "pop-beer," or cheap jewelry. Games of chance beckoned those willing to risk a few coins. There were little tents in which "strange people" and "wonders of nature" could be viewed. These sideshows offered fat women, skeletal men, albino boys, or six-legged calves, whatever might catch the attention of the curious.

Inside the circus tent—it cost twenty-five cents to enter and perhaps another quarter for a seat—performing men, women, and children rode horses, turned somersaults, leaped barriers, and climbed long poles held by an "understander." There were people who walked on tightropes, contorted themselves into pretzel shapes, or hurled cannonballs into the air and caught them on their necks and shoulders. All these feats were done to the accompaniment of a small brass band.

When the performance, ended the spectators congregated outside the tent in a convivial meeting; it was only three or four o'clock in the afternoon. They picnicked again, ran races, wrestled, and engaged in all the kinds of activity that any holiday engendered. At dark, they hitched up their teams and set out for home.

These circus-day scenes were not only played out in Wisconsin, of course, but were repeated across the country, and had been for years. As with the Fourth of July, the county fair, militia musterings, and election day, the visit of a circus was a genuine holiday for everyone. The first show to perform in Wisconsin arrived in 1843. From then until the advent of radio broadcasting, the circus was the premier entertainment for the citizens of the state, as it was everywhere.

Of circus people themselves, Wisconsin had a full measure, both famous and obscure. The Mabie brothers, the Ringling brothers, William C. Coup, the Holland family, and Burr Robbins were well known as owners of large, successful circuses. There were others, those whose shows visited the small towns and hamlets and who are nearly forgotten today. These include George Hall, the Skerbecks, and the Wintermute brothers, all of whom are treated in this volume.

These rolls could be carried on for many pages: the cities of Delavan, Baraboo, Evansville, and Appleton by themselves can contribute many names to the history of the circus and to the honor of the state of Wisconsin. In sum, the contribution to all facets of American enterprise includes a healthy portion of Wisconsin citizens who spent their working lives entertaining men, women, and children through this unique institution.

INTRODUCTION

Horses had been pulling circuses from town to town for twenty years before one got as far west as Wisconsin. Based as they were in the East, the circus showmen had to wait upon settlement, upon the formation of audiences, before they could reach the western states. As the river valleys and crossroads became populated, the tented circuses reached out to them, as did the freight haulers, the innkeepers, and the postal service. After the War of 1812 and the breaching of the Appalachian barrier, there was a great migration westward, and the entertainers followed along. The first circus in Pittsburgh is dated 1814; in Cincinnati, 1815. But these were not tented shows. They were presented in temporary buildings or theatres, as all circuses had been since the first American circus took place in Philadelphia in 1793.

When the earliest circuses performed in buildings, the showmen needed a large population from which to draw an audience. This necessity limited them to the cities, and most of the cities were on or near the Atlantic coast. It wasn't until 1825 that two New York showmen had a canvas tent manufactured that could cover a forty-two-foot circus ring and a few hundred standing spectators. This innovation changed the circus forever. With the introduction of the tent came itinerancy, and circuses were free to go where they wished, wherever an audience might be expected. Whereas the semipermanent arena circuses played in one city for several weeks or even several months, the tented shows could stop in a village for a day or two, pack up, and move on. Thus was the circus genre introduced to a broad spectrum of the national, as well as Canadian, population.

Samuel H. Nichols was most likely the earliest showman to advertise in Wisconsin. (There might have been earlier ones, but our research is limited to newspaper advertisements and therefore is dependent on newspaper survival.) Nichols was the proprietor of a tented circus in 1838 based in Albany, New York. In that year he made a tour of New Jersey and Pennsylvania. In the next season he journeyed as far west as Wooster, Ohio, returning to Albany in the fall. In 1840 he hardly strayed out of New York State, possibly as a result of the expense he incurred building an arena in Albany, but in both 1841 and 1842 he got as far west as Cleveland. Instead of returning to New York for the hibernal months of 1842, he wintered over in Ohio, most likely in Zanesville. Thus placed, he could start in the spring for points even farther west. He was in Chicago on August 4, 1843, and on August 11 reached Racine, Wisconsin.

Journeys such as those Nichols made, on poor roads or no roads, in all types of weather, mostly at night, were the lot of the wagon-borne circus troupes of the era. Comments handed down by those who were part of it run to the same complaints. It was a very fatiguing grind. They were roused out of bed at anywhere from two to five a.m., depending on the length of the morning's drive. It was hard and dirty work for the laborers. The food—usually salt pork and boiled potatoes—was acceptable or not, depending on the innkeeper's efforts. The jolting rides over poorly maintained roads were not without incident; mudholes threatened to swallow the wagons, swollen streams had to be forded. It was not unusual for everyone to climb down from the wagons and walk several miles to relieve the horses on steep hills or bottomless roads. These events were doubly miserable in rainstorms or on dark nights. Quite often the path itself would be lost. Though it became ritualized, the daily trek was anything but predictable.

Arriving at the day's place of performance, be it a village, a crossroads, or a country store, the workmen would raise the tent and assemble the seats, then repair to the hotel for breakfast. The second section, consisting of buggies and carryalls that transported the staff and performers, would halt at a distance from town. Here the circus people would change into costumes, mount their ring horses, climb into the bandwagon, and parade in on the main street, ending at the circus lot. The average tent was a hundred feet in diameter and held 2,000 persons. The performance lasted two to three hours and was given but once in small venues, twice in larger towns.

There were riders, both male and female; acrobats; clowns; and sometimes jugglers and weight lifters. Half the programs were horse acts. A few songs were interspersed, and some shows ended with a "laughable farce," a comedy act or burlesque. All this was accompanied by the circus band, made up of three to ten musicians, brass instruments predominating.

The circus was one of the few and certainly the largest of the live entertainments to reach the rural public, which found it highly entertaining. The displays of horseflesh, the muscular dexterity of the athletes, and even the antics of the clowns appealed to the largely inhibited and credulous audience.

Unlike when it was introduced to the eastern states, the circus was a known quantity to the early settlers of Wisconsin. These settlers were Americans from New York State and New England and had been exposed to the institution in their native places. The great foreign immigration into the Great Lakes area was just beginning when Sam Nichols reached Racine. The circus in Europe was an urban entertainment, so the peasant-farmers from Germany who migrated to America had to be educated in its pleasures, but fortunately for the showmen their product was not an intellectual pursuit and was easily understood.

After Nichols's 1843 visit, southeastern Wisconsin saw at least one circus in each succeeding season. They were all of the wagon-borne type we have just described, having fifteen to twenty wagons, fifty or so horses, and ten to fifteen performers. With minor variations their programs were identical.

There were two main paths for entrance into the state. One led out of Chicago north along the shore of Lake Michigan. This one encompassed Waukegan, Kenosha, Racine, and Milwaukee. The other followed the Rock River valley through Beloit, Janesville, and

Watertown. These were the main areas of settlement, of course, and it was population that drew the showmen. It was common for the troupes to go from Chicago up to Milwaukee, then move west to the Rock River and follow it south into Illinois.

A third group of villages also attracted the shows—the lead-mining venues in the southwestern corner of the state. Though the population was spread over a wide area, some settlements saw circuses before 1850, Dodgeville, Mineral Point, Platteville, and Hazel Green among them. Companies that visited these places were more than likely on their way to Galena and Dubuque, and because of the nature of their travel, having to perform every day but Sunday to cover daily expenses, stopped in mining towns on their way through.

The popularity of these early circuses in Wisconsin is attested to by the fact that the same companies undertook the travails of the roads, and lack of roads, year after year. Willard R. Smith, writing in the *Milwaukee Journal*, pointed out that when the first field show—actually a menagerie—visited Madison in 1848, the first state legislature adjourned so that the members could attend.

In both 1845 and 1846 the Howes & Mabie circus reached Wisconsin, which led in turn to the founding of the first winter quarters to be established in the state, an event we will discuss in Chapter 1.

MABIE BROTHERS

The physical establishment of the circus in Wisconsin began with a purchase of land near Delavan in June 1847 by Edmund Mabie, who with his brother Jeremiah operated E. F. & J. Mabie's Grand Olympic Arena and United States Circus. The brothers had quartered their company in St. Louis during the preceding two winters after traveling extensively in the West. They bought the property in Wisconsin with the purpose of using it for a permanent winter quarters.

From this location their circus was able to visit Missouri, Illinois, and Iowa early in their summer tours, before the eastern shows, departing from New York and Philadelphia, could reach the western towns. Thus, the Mabies' appearances had little or no opposition until July or August. We don't know how long the Mabie brothers had been planning to do this, but they were the first to make such a move, not only in Wisconsin but in the entire western portion of the country.

Other circuses had wintered away from the traditional eastern bases, but these were all of a temporary nature. The Mabies were the first to purchase land and construct buildings to house their animals and properties. Using what buildings were already on the 400 acres—part of it had been the property of a horse dealer—the showmen spent the winter of 1847–1848 in Delavan and opened their 1848 season there. They needed grass for the horses, abundant fuel to heat the animal houses, and mechanics to repair their equipment, all of which Delavan could provide.

Edmund (1810–1867) and Jeremiah (1812–1867) Mabie were the sons of Joshua and Elizabeth Gifford Mabie and were but two of that couple's eleven children, born in Putnam County, New York, near the village of Patterson. They were farmers until they were in their thirties, when they copied so many of their Putnam County neighbors and went into the circus business. Putnam and Westchester counties in New York have since been called the cradle of the American circus, because so many of the early showmen came from that area. This is especially true of menagerie owners. When farmers realized how much money they could make by traveling about the country exhibiting wild beasts—this was in the 1820s and 1830s—farms were mortgaged and bank notes guaranteed to provide investment in field shows.

The Mabies were such investors in 1841. They made a wise choice by forming a partnership with an established showman, Nathan A. Howes. By 1841 Howes (1796–1878) had been entertaining the public for thirty years. At fifteen he learned rope walking from an itinerant performer, who paid him a dollar a day to travel with him. In 1826 he was a partner with Aaron Turner and Sylvester Reynolds in a show that had a canvas tent, the second circus in

The older of the two Mabie showmen, Edmund moved to Delavan and became an important member of the community. He married star performer Laura Buckley, who promptly retired from the ring. Carte de visite, undated, courtesy Charles G. Spooner.

the world to own such a structure. In the ensuing seasons Howes was very active in the business. He trained his younger brothers, Wilson and Seth B., to be riders, and they were with him for years. His longest association was with Richard Sands, one of the outstanding performers of the era. They had circuses on the road for seven years, the last one in 1840.

The New York Circus, sometimes advertised as the Olympic Circus, was under the management of S. B. Howes & Co. Since neither the Mabies nor Nathan Howes was on the payroll, but Seth B. Howes was (to the tune of $2,335.70 for the tour), we assume he was the hired manager. There were about thirty-five people in the company, nearly half of whom were performers. Relatives of the Mabies, Sylvester and Marlin, possibly brothers, were the agents. The 1841 season opened in Patterson on April 15, and the Mabies began circus careers that were to last until 1865.

Nathan Howes must not have approved of his brother's management in 1841, as in 1842 he took over as manager and relegated Seth B. Howes to the post of equestrian director. As in the first year, the route chosen wound through New England and eastern Canada. Seth B. Howes (1815–1901) was the star performer.

Apparently satisfied with his stint as manager, Nate Howes bowed out of the firm for 1843, taking out another circus, called Howes & Gardner. Jeremiah Mabie also took a one-year sabbatical from the show. Thus S. B. Howes and E. F. Mabie were listed as managers and proprietors. It was in this year that Howes & Mabie first ventured into the western states. They crossed New York, went by lake steamer from Buffalo to Detroit, and visited Michigan, Indiana, and Illinois. Then, in another departure, they played the Mississippi River towns as far as New Orleans, which they reached on December 14. They set up at Conde and Hospital streets, where they performed until January 11. It was not unusual in the antebellum period for circuses to travel year-round; some sixty percent did so. The return on investment in a successful operation was so great that wintering off the road was almost an indulgence.

Though he traveled with, and sometimes managed, the Mabie circus and menagerie, Jeremiah Mabie chose to retain interests in Putnam County, New York, whence the family originated. Print, undated, courtesy Dorothy LaBar and Wayne Landerholm.

Leaving New Orleans in January 1844, the troupe went to Mobile, Alabama, then through Georgia as far as Savannah, and up to Charleston. By June they had crossed the Carolinas and entered Virginia. This is as far east as they penetrated, and they were not to do so again until 1857. Both Mabies and Seth B. Howes were present on this trek. They visited Kentucky and Tennessee and returned through Georgia and Alabama to Mobile, where they exhibited from December to February 1845.

After a month's stay in New Orleans they traveled upriver to St. Louis, which they reached in early April 1845. They toured the Midwest until September and then went to Kentucky, St. Louis, and again down to New Orleans. November was spent in the Crescent City, and then they returned north, apparently not performing over the winter.

It was in 1846 that Seth B. Howes sold out his interest in the circus. This was in September, or at least his name still appeared in the advertising at that time. Howes & Co., a large eastern circus, was on the road in the same year, and it appears that S. B. Howes & Co. was operating it; perhaps Nathan Howes was the "& Co." In any event it was Seth's property over the next three seasons. It could be that discussions concerning a permanent location in the West were already under way and that Howes was not interested in the idea.

To replace Seth B. Howes, who had been the leading rider since the inception of the company in 1841, the Mabies hired Harry Buckley and his family (father Matthew as clown, sister Laura as equestrienne). The Buckleys began their duties in March 1846 at the season-opening stand in St. Louis, so Seth Howes may have ended his riding career by then. The parting was amicable. For several seasons various performers from the Howeses' circuses went west to appear with the Mabies, presumably recommended by Howes.

In 1847 the title of the company was changed from New York Circus and Olympic Arena to Grand Olympic Arena and United States Circus, perhaps to show more universality. Edmund Mabie was the manager in both 1847 and 1848. And, of course, it was in June of 1847 that the first purchase of property in Delavan was made. They opened, as usual, in St. Louis and had a strictly western route in 1847, touching on Illinois, Wisconsin, Iowa, Missouri, and Indiana. They were to follow this pattern until late in 1851. It was in 1848 that the Holland Family troupe joined the show; they later moved to Delavan and became important figures in local circus history.

Jeremiah Mabie managed the company in 1849, probably because Edmund was busy with the Delavan property. From then on it is apparent that the brothers spent less time traveling with the company. Pardon A. Older (1819–1908), a man with no experience in the business, traded his sawmill in Janesville, Wisconsin, for a one-third interest in the Mabie concern in this year. He valued the mill at $5,000, and by our reckoning paid just twice what a third of the circus was worth. However, he was also buying into a daily gross of at least $100. It was a small outfit, consisting of twenty horses, eight wagons, an eighty-five-foot main tent, and a thirty-foot dressing tent. The opening stand was in Chicago, the closing one in St. Louis, where the winter quarters were established.

Edmund Mabie was the manager again in 1850. They opened and closed the season in St. Louis and wintered there as well. Why they did not use the Delavan quarters remains a mystery; it could be that the buildings were not yet adequate for their needs. After using the property in the winter of 1847–1848, they did not do so again until 1854. One advantage to opening in St. Louis mir-

A single action-filled engraving brought the reader's eye to circus ads. All the features presented by the circus were described in accurate terms; exaggerated written and visual hyperbole would become common in a few years. Newspaper advertisement, 1847, Circus World Museum.

rored their choice of a western base, as the eastern shows couldn't get that far west that early. Until 1851 no circus appeared in St. Louis earlier than the Mabie company. Usually one to three months separated Mabie's opening stand and the appearance of the next show. St. Louis was a "good show town," and the Mabies' customary two-week stand filled the company's coffers, getting the season started on a profitable basis.

At the end of the usual Midwestern tour in 1851, H. A. Woodward, the agent, was replaced by Samuel B. DeLand, who was familiar with southern trouping. He guided the company from Missouri into Arkansas, and farther south. When he reached St. Louis on the trip back north, he in turn was replaced by William Davis for the summer tour. This was one of the earliest such arrangements thus far discovered. The practice of hiring agents with specific knowledge of the area to be toured became common on most circuses in the years to come. Familiarity with the country and with local officials made an agent valuable to a circus owner.

Pardon A. Older, who had been learning the business since becoming a partner in 1849, became the manager in 1852. In his honor the title was changed when the troupe left St. Louis. It became the Great United States Circus of Older & Co. This lasted until November and the annual winter southern tour.

James Raymond was the leading menagerie impresario of the nineteenth century. It had become the habit of his heirs to attach their large menagerie to circuses on a lease basis. The usual arrangement was to leave the management of these combinations to the circus compa-

Pardon A. Older entered the circus business with the Mabies in 1849 and remained active through 1884. In late 1872 he operated a circus in the South bearing the name of P. T. Barnum. Trade card, 1872, Joseph T. Bradbury Gift, Circus World Museum.

ny. The advantage was that the circus could have a menagerie without the expense of purchasing one. Further, by being able to use the well-known menagerie titles—Raymond, Van Amburgh, Driesbach—the advertising was much enhanced.

The Mabies entered into such a contract in November 1852 by which their move south was made under the cumbersome title of Mabie & Co.'s United States Circus and Raymond & Co. and Driesbach & Co.'s Menageries Combined. Pardon A. Older was still the manager. By this arrangement the Mabies, for the first time, traveled with an elephant. Having such a beast with a circus added a certain cachet. After a July 1853 stand in St. Louis, the Raymond name was dropped from the title. Driesbach had retired by this season, and the lions were put to work under George Beasley, who used the stage name Signor Hideralgo. Beasley was to stay with Mabie from then until he retired after the 1859 tour, first as trainer and then as menagerie superintendent.

The circus–menagerie combination must have been remunerative, as the 1854 season found the Mabies with another attached menagerie. This group of animals had been on Richard Sands's circus in 1853 and were brought west by the famous rider John J. Nathans, who remained with the Mabies as equestrian manager. Nathans was one of Sands's partners. Six lions were turned over to Beasley, and the elephant, Romeo, was under the care of Herr Hoonsinger. There were at least eighteen other animals plus monkeys and birds in the collection. P. A. Older sold his third of the firm back to the Mabie brothers in 1854, and S. B. DeLand became the manager. The circus returned from its southern trip in April, and the menagerie was added at that time. After the usual Midwestern tour the circus acts were discharged in Quincy, Illinois, in October, and the menagerie, now titled E. F. & J. Mabie's Grand Combined Menagerie, went through Missouri, Arkansas, and Texas, ending up at New Orleans in February 1855. Both this and the 1854 tours of the South were accomplished by steamboat transportation for at least a portion of each trip.

The circus spent the summer months of 1855 in Iowa, Missouri, and Illinois. In November the menagerie was combined with a circus and a troupe of Native American Indians to form what was called Mabie's Menagerie, Den Stone's Circus & Tyler's Indian Exhibition. Such a lengthy title was not at all unusual in the early nineteenth century. The thinking seems to have been that the longer the title, the grander the exhibition. Dennison Stone, well-known clown, had a nine-man circus contingent, and Tyler had seven Seneca Indians. They had been attached to Van Amburgh's Menagerie that summer and were contracted by the Mabies when Van Amburgh closed for the season. They combined in Louisville, where the Bruce Wagon Company of Cincinnati delivered a new set of wagons, and set off for Tennessee, Alabama, and Georgia. S. B. DeLand was still manager for the Mabies. Returning north in 1856, the company spent a week in May exhibiting in St. Louis, and it was here that they took delivery of the first Mabie-owned elephants.

Seth B. Howes had been P. T. Barnum's partner in the operation of a traveling show from 1851 through 1854. This company had seven elephants, the most on any field show to that

MABIE'S GRAND MENAGERIE!

And Moral Exhibition,

Of the marvels and splendors of Animated Nature, organized for the season of 1863, is the most extensive, complete and magnificent establishment of the kind extant. Language is inadequate to perfectly describe.

Elephant teams were a great feature of menagerie and circus parades. The first was James Raymond's four "bull" hitch of 1843. The Mabie team had five beasts in 1856 and possibly six in later years. Newspaper advertisement, 1863, Circus World Museum.

time. When Barnum auctioned the chattels in 1854, Howes bought all seven of the pachyderms, which Howes in turn auctioned at the end of the 1855 season with the rest of his menagerie. Edmund Mabie bought four of the beasts, paying $4,700. They were shipped to St. Louis for the May 1856 stand. Mabie already had the elephant Romeo on lease from the Sands interests. Thus, the company paraded their bandwagon in St. Louis with a five-elephant hitch. This practice was maintained for the balance of the season as they toured Missouri, Iowa, and Wisconsin. With such an attraction and a doubling of the size of their circus contingent, plus Tyler's Indians, the Mabies had increased their circus to the point where they could match the large eastern shows feature for feature.

Mabie's Grand Consolidated Menagerie and Circus left Delavan in May 1857, not to return there for four years. (This was not an unusual thing to do; there is record of a circus being on the road continuously for eleven years.) Over that time the company would stop for week or so and, while performing each day, would do maintenance on the equipment, replace tired horses with fresh ones, hire new artists, and bid goodbye to others. In December 1857 they spent a week in Charleston pursuing such activities. In 1859 and 1860 they had similar stays in St. Louis.

Samuel B. DeLand was manager during the first two years of the sojourn. Jerry Mabie took over active management in 1859, and it appears that DeLand returned for 1860. Mabie, who spent most of his time in New York, would join the show once in a while to see how things were being handled.

The trail led to the southeastern states, back across the South to Texas (1858), and upriver to Missouri and into Kansas (where they'd never been). This was in 1859, and from Kansas they went east and then south to Texas again (1860), and finally upriver to Wisconsin and home. By this time the *Cincinnati Daily Commercial* had several times remarked that the show appeared tired, time-worn, and ancient.

They left Delavan in 1857 with the four elephants from Howes. Romeo had been returned to the Sands partners. During the season one of the elephants died, so they made do with three, which was still more than most circuses carried. The large menagerie they had acquired from Sands was still with them, though it must have been much depleted by 1860.

The connection between the Mabies and the Sands interests (Richard Sands, J. J. Nathans, Avery Smith, and Gerard Quick), which dated back to the 1854 lease or purchase of the Sands animals, must have been the result of Jeremiah Mabie's presence in New York and his predilection for mingling with the eastern show-men. We have seen that J. J. Nathans joined the Mabie circus for the 1854 tour. From that point the involvement of the Mabies themselves lessened. They ceased to be the day-to-day managers. Edmund was active in Delavan, as we will discuss further, and Jeremiah, as we mentioned, spent most of his time in New York. Selling an interest to P. A. Older and allowing him to manage, forming the partnership with the Raymond interests, and other activities all lead us to the conclusion that the brothers were allowing their capital to work rather than being completely involved themselves.

In 1858 the Mabies financed or supplied the equipment for a second troupe, called Mabie & Crosby's French and American Circus. It was framed in Lewistown, Pennsylvania, and managed by Orlando Crosby. From Lewistown it crossed Pennsylvania, went into Ohio and Illinois, and ended its season in St. Louis. In 1859 it went on tour as Davis & Crosby. This change in ownership may have meant that Crosby had paid off the Mabies, which is why we suggest that their interest was financial.

J. J. Nathans came west to manage the company again in 1861. The title in that year was E. F. & J. Mabie and J. J. Nathans Combined. The War of the Rebellion and the circus season both began in April. The effect on field shows was immediate, but not crippling. They had lost half of their usual territory, and some substituted for that by touring in Canada. Nathans guided the show into Ontario after crossing southern Michigan. It was the first time the Mabie name had been north of the border since the brothers' partnership with S. B. Howes in 1846. They crossed Ontario (then called Upper Canada) from Detroit and back, and then went into Ohio and Indiana. Business

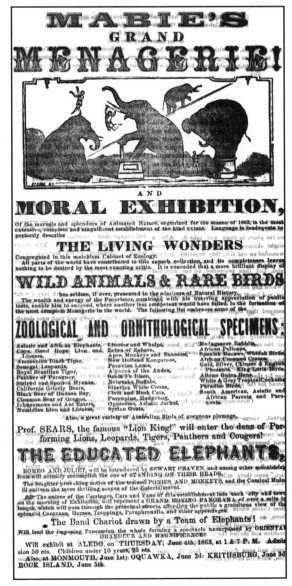

The Mabie menagerie, a veritable traveling zoo, presented a wide variety of species to its patrons, along with a number of circus acts in a ring. Elephants were already a circus icon in the 1850s. Newspaper advertisement, 1863, Circus World Museum.

was generally bad for circuses in 1861, as might be expected given the more serious concerns of the populace, but the Mabies decided to mount a project they had never attempted. They opened a winter show in Chicago. The old Washington Street lot, across from the Court House (and between two churches), was rented and a heated pavilion constructed. They played there until May 10, 1862, and launched their summer tour from there on May 12. Nathans had gone back east, and the circus went out as Mabie's Great Show.

The company stayed close to home in 1862, visiting Ohio, Illinois, Iowa, and Wisconsin, and were back in Delavan on November 1. This was the second season in a row that they played Ohio, a state they had avoided over the years because of its popularity with the eastern circuses. As we said, circus territory was confined because of the war, and it was for that reason the Mabies went to Ohio in 1861 and 1862.

Once again they had a winter show in Chicago, this one on the same lot as before, beginning November 13. When they paid the performers on January 10, 1863, it was for the last time, as they had no circus acts for the remaining two years under Mabie ownership. Mabie's Grand Menagerie was the new title. They opened in Delavan on May 1 and closed in Chicago on November 3. Again, the route was closely confined to the Midwestern states. The menagerie was a large one and featured trained elephants and a lion act, but no riders or acrobats.

For the 1863 season we have the only financial records found for a Mabie tour. Tickets for the main show were sold for the amount of $107,000. Concert, or after-show, sales were $1,700. Privilege men paid for the "privilege" of traveling with a circus while conducting their own work. They might have sideshows, or refreshment stands, or novelty sales. The gambling games and shortchange artistry that some circuses allowed were also privileges. The Mabie sideshow privilege was contracted out at $100 per week and the concessions stand for $40 per week. Two other privileges (possibly stands on the grounds) brought in $2,000. All this yielded a gross of about $113,000 (1991 equivalent, $1,484,820). The largest daily expense was about $100 for hotels (only the workmen slept on the lot). Fifty cents a day was the workmen's pay, though some of the staff made as much as $50 a week. If the show had been a circus instead of a menagerie, the payroll would have been much higher.

Most likely seeking open spaces, away from the glut of circuses in Indiana and Illinois—there were six shows in each in 1863—Jerry Mabie decreed a more western route for 1864. P. A. Older, once again the manager, took the road to Iowa, Minnesota, and Nebraska. The Mabies had never played in the latter two

Tony Pastor, who later rose to prominence in the vaudeville business, clowned with the 1857 Mabie and 1858 Mabie & Crosby troupes. Clad in decorated body-hugging wardrobe, humorous monologues and singing characterized the buffoon's presentations in that time. Photograph, undated, courtesy The Harvard Theatre Collection, The Houghton Library.

domains. It was a different country, an area of bad roads and sparse population. Only three places in the season lured them into a two-day stand—St. Paul, Minnesota; St. Joseph, Missouri; and Leavenworth, Kansas. On August 2 in Council Bluffs, Iowa, a windstorm destroyed the main tent, and they used a side-walled arena for a week awaiting a new big top. It didn't arrive until August 24. "Mabie was not fit to be around," an employee noted. With the new tent they went on for two more weeks, when Mabie gave orders to turn around and start back. He had had enough of "the west and wide open spaces." They crossed Iowa, plagued by bad weather. In mid-October they reached Delavan and unloaded the wagons. It marked the end of the Mabie show.

This recital of the years and the routes of Wisconsin's first circus is devoid of the most important element of its success—the people who filled its rosters. In such a peripatetic type of organization as a circus, a group gathered in the spring and dispersed in the winter; there is nothing to connect one year to the next, barring the owners themselves. Yet the Mabies had a high percentage of people who adhered to their colors season after season. Many came from Delavan itself; many came there for employment and stayed. This would indicate that they were treated well and that their salaries were adequate. We cannot name them all, but those with long attachment are worthy of our mention. Luke Tilden spent fifteen years with the Mabies, starting as a workman and rising to an administrative position. Walter Waterman, a two- and four-horse rider, had a long career with the Mabies. It amounted to ten years, a very long association. (The average performer's stint with one circus was two years.) In 1863 Waterman was paid $55 per week (1991 equivalent, $715). William M. Davis, who served as agent and manager at various times, likewise was with the company for ten years. Harry Buckley, the rider, and George Beasley, the lion trainer, were each present for seven years. The rider James DeMott and the elephant trainer Stewart Craven lasted six years. N. Colson led the Mabie band for five seasons.

The principal riders, always the star performers in wagon show days, were men of progressively higher talent as the years went by. This was because, as the show grew and income increased, higher salaries could be offered. In the days of Howes & Mabie (1841–1846) Seth B. Howes was the principal rider. When the Mabies parted from him, they hired Henry "Harry" Buckley, who had understudied Howes in 1846. He was but seventeen years old but had been riding for eleven years. The son of Matthew Buckley, formerly a clown but now the Mabie ringmaster, he was presumably the most accomplished rider in the West. Buckley held the position through the season of 1852.

Others who worked for the Mabies were Davis Richards in 1853, J. J. Nathans in 1854, and William Pastor in 1857. Beginning in 1858, James DeMott was the principal rider for three seasons, and in 1862 the premier horseman, James Melville, probably the most talented of all these men, was

Stewart Craven was America's foremost elephant trainer in the mid-nineteenth century. His enlightened training style, based on a profound understanding of animals, contrasted with the subjugation methodology of others. Photograph, undated, Circus World Museum.

the headliner. As the roster grew, there were hurdle riders, scenic riders, and two- and four-horse riders that complemented the principal rider. In the earlier years Harry Buckley filled all these roles by himself.

The equestriennes with the show (again, after Howes had parted) began with Laura Buckley, Matthew's daughter and Harry's sister. She was the only female with the troupe from 1846 to 1848. She married Edmund Mabie in 1850 and retired from performing. Women performers were not universally approved of by antebellum audiences. The idea of a woman traveling about the countryside with an element not socially acceptable itself was in sharp opposition to the traditional idea of "a woman's place." Because of this sentiment, women who did appear in the circus were almost always sisters, daughters, or wives of men in the companies. It was not unusual for circus advertisements to assure the public that no females were with the troupe. (The Mabies themselves did this in Kansas in 1859.) John Wells, the clown, was engaged by the Mabie show in 1849 and 1850. His four daughters, all performers, traveled with him and graced several circuses in the period. Women who performed with the Mabies included Marietta Zanfretta, a feature rider in 1852; Emma Nathans (Emma C. Paulin), J. J. Nathan's stepdaughter, in 1854; a Mademoiselle Leaman in 1857; and Fannie Jamison in 1858–1859.

A review of the rosters over the years discloses no performers of particular brilliance among the clowns and acrobats that made up the rest of the lists. In this regard, the Mabies could be considered as having an average group of performers. Perhaps the most surprising thing about the company was the number of innovations in circus operation that it fostered. These didn't necessarily come from the Mabies themselves, but their willingness to accept changes indicates a certain open-mindedness unusual among their largely conservative brethren.

The first of these, of course, was the decision to locate permanently in the West. This was quite possibly the making of the Mabie fortunes. The importance of the ability to cover the burgeoning Midwestern territory early in the year, before the circuses coming out of New York and Pennsylvania could reach such places, cannot be overstressed. It made the Mabie circus the preeminent western field show, despite its lack of size in the earlier years.

Less important, but historically significant, was the introduction of the first cookhouse, or captive kitchen, and the Mabie outfit being the first field show to provide sleeping facilities on the circus lot. These innovations were begun in 1858. They were a direct reflection of the increasing size of traveling companies in the years before the Civil War.

From the beginning of tented touring, employees had been lodged and fed in hotels along the route. When the performers and workmen numbered only about thirty people, the cost and availability of such accommodations were not a major consideration. A man and a horse could be fed and housed for as little as fifty cents or as much as a dollar a day depending on the local price structure. This sum provided two meals and half a bed for the man and feed, straw, and stabling for the animal. As the size of rosters expanded in the 1850s, these costs became of increasing concern. Also, especially in the West and South, the availability of facilities in small towns became problematic. Most hotels could put up twenty or so guests, two to a room; thus a circus company was forced to use several hotels if they arrived with a hundred employees and as many horses. One solution was to spread straw on the floor of a room, nail a tarpaulin over it, and let as many workmen as possible squeeze into the space. A better solution, arrived at on the Mabie show, was to feed and house the workmen on the lot. Staff and performers still used hotels.

William M. Davis Jr., manager of the circus from 1857 through 1860, claimed credit for the idea of a "camp outfit" ("camp" was the contemporary term for "circus lot"). He wrote, "I prevailed on the Mabies to get a cooking outfit and sleeping and horse tents, contending that sooner or later all shows would be compelled to do similarly." Accepting the advice, Jerry Mabie went to the Vandiveer tent company in Cincinnati and ordered a camp outfit consisting of sleeping tents for seventy people, a dining tent, a cook wagon, and horse tents. The cost was $1,500, and the savings over a season have been projected at close to $5,000.

Pink lemonade was introduced on the Mabie show, though it had little to do with the firm itself. Peter Conklin, who operated a peanut and lemonade stand on the Mabie lot, said he originated it, and we have found no other claimants to the honor. In a 1911 interview in the *New York Clipper*, Conklin said it happened in Texas in 1857, but he was notorious for misdating his memories. Circumstances, as outlined by him, point to early 1859 as the birth of the hued beverage. Nominally a clown with the circus—his first such effort—Conklin had resigned because of a salary dispute. Not wanting to leave the show because his brother was still with it, Pete bought two mules and a spring wagon, some peanuts, sugar, tartaric, and one lemon and set up a candy stand. He ran out of water one day, in a place where there were no wells and no creek. He went into the tents and in the dressing tent found Fannie Jamison, the rider, wringing out a pair of pink tights into a bucket. He took the bucket, pink water and all, and poured it into his lemonade tub. He started shouting, "Strawberry lemonade!" and a classic tradition was born.

Though his skills as a singing clown are long forgotten, Pete Conklin's position in circus history is secure because of his invention of pink lemonade. Two brothers, George and John, were long-term circus men. Engraving, June 2, 1866, New York Clipper.

That the Mabie brothers' circus was a successful operation from beginning to end cannot be doubted. For seventeen years they traveled the West and South, and as far as is known from the scant records that survived, they never had an unprofitable season. The Mabies themselves were astute businessmen; what little we know of their personalities includes descriptions of them as close-mouthed and tight-fisted. When they established their head-quarters outside Delavan, the local populace received them guardedly, not because of their actions, but because they were circus men. Edmund Mabie overcame these prejudices by involving himself in the life of the village. He and his brother purchased the Delavan Milling Company, said by one commentator to be the largest business in the county. A few years later the brothers accepted P. A. Older's mill in

Janesville, trading a third-interest in the circus. Edmund helped in the development of a plank road through Delavan to Racine. He pledged $2,500 to the arrangement whereby the Racine & Mississippi Railroad changed its route some two-and-a-half miles in order to pass through Delavan. Later, he was elected a trustee of the village and was a director of the Walworth County Agricultural Society.

These civic efforts involved Jeremiah Mabie only as an investor, as he retained his residence in Putnam County, New York. Neither brother was married until they were forty years of age. Both married teenaged wives, the custom at the time, and both had families. Edmund and his wife, Laura Buckley, had eight children; Jeremiah and Anna Mary Field had three. The brothers died within two months of each other in 1867.

Their public legacy lay within circus history, as we've delineated here, and their efforts on behalf of Delavan opened that village to a period of growth and fame.

DELAVAN'S CIRCUS COLONY

With the establishment at Delavan of the Mabie winter quarters there began a process known to many villages. This was the gradual migration of persons seeking employment in a local industry. If the Mabies had been wagon builders, they would have attracted carpenters, wheelwrights, and blacksmiths. Since they were circus owners they brought in their wake performers, trainers, grooms, and the like. Edmund Mabie himself was the first of the circus people to settle in Delavan, then came Matthew Buckley's family, and then that of John Holland. All the children of these families became performers in the years ahead. In this manner the circus community in Delavan grew, made up not only of newcomers, but also of Delavanites who participated in the institution for varying periods of time.

A visitor to the site of the Mabie brothers' winter quarters on Lake Delavan cannot but be struck by the beauty of the landscape. The lake and its surrounding greenery, though impacted to a degree by subsequent settlement, remains one of the most attractive vistas in Wisconsin. It was this abundant grassland and water that Edmund Mabie saw as a fine place for their permanent quarters, since those features were nearly perfect for grazing their horses. "We are on the very pitch of a fine prairie where everything flourishes," Matthew Buckley wrote to Jeremiah Mabie, who was in New York. "(Edmund) has beat me in buying land though we have got almost 1,000 acres between us with buildings and good fences." They paid nine dollars an acre for the property, which only a few years before was sold by the federal government for a dollar and a quarter. The "good fences" added to both the desirability and the price.

Buckley (1800–1897), who had been with the Howes & Mabie company in 1846, was the first of the circus performers to move to Delavan. He was the equestrian manager and ringmaster for the troupe, retiring at the end of 1849, after thirty-nine years as a performer and proprietor. With him were his sons, Henry ("Harry") and Edward, and daughters, Laura and Harriett. A third son, James, was born in Delavan in 1848. Matthew and his wife, Marianne, lived in the village for the rest of their lives.

Harry Buckley (1829–1884) was, as we mentioned, the principal rider for the Mabie circus, replacing Seth B. Howes in 1846. It was the principal rider who was the star of any show. He was the man who leaped the garters and burst the paper-covered hoops and generally cavorted while standing on the back of his circling horse. To hold this position at the age of seventeen reflected well on Harry's proficiency, and no doubt on his father's tutelage as well. He was over six feet tall and weighed over 200 pounds, very large for a principal rider, most of whom were five-something and about 135 pounds.

British-born Matthew Buckley contributed to the origination of Delavan as a circus community. He amazed local residents by doing a back somersault on his 90th birthday, and lived another seven years beyond the feat. Photograph, undated, courtesy Gordon Yadon.

It was Harry who organized the first circus to originate in Delavan (and thus in Wisconsin). This was in 1856. He last rode for the Mabies in 1852, then spent three years with the L. G. Butler company, a Chicago circus. On May 3, 1856, H. Buckley & Co.'s National Circus had its first performance, suitably in Delavan. With eleven performers, which included the proprietor, the company set out on a six-month tour that touched Wisconsin, Iowa, and Illinois.

By 1856, organizing a circus had become rather routine. Wagon builders in Delavan could supply the vehicle needs. To obtain new tenting Buckley would have had to go to Chicago sailmakers. Of course, he could buy used tents, possibly from the Mabies. Horses were in plentiful supply. Nicholas Thorne, the man who sold a portion of the Delavan Lake property to Edmund Mabie, was a horse dealer in Delavan. And hiring workmen would not be difficult. Many of them simply appeared in circus towns every spring, much like migrant farm laborers. Delavanites would hire on for a season, just to taste the life.

Arranging for staff and performers was a matter of letter writing and of using the grapevine. Buckley's confreres in the L. G. Butler Circus supplied his manager, Oscar Hyatt; his equestrian director, Walter Waterman; and his acrobats, the Holland family. One clown, Tony Parker, had been with the Mabies.

Buckley's 1857 effort was an expansion of the first year's operation, both in the size of the circus and in its extended route. He had two partners, Stephen S. Babcock and George Passage. Babcock was a Delavan grocer who later became a circus advance agent. Several persons who later would make a mark in the business were with the show. John A. Dingess, the agent, had been with Mabie in 1856; George S. Cole, the treasurer, would go from Buckley to Mabie in 1861; George Orrin and his sons were acrobats who later established permanent circuses in Havana and Mexico City; W. W. Cole, who spent his first year in the business with Buckley, would later own major field shows; Cole's mother, Mary Ann Cook Cole, was a rider with Buckley.

The itinerary included Iowa, Illinois, and Indiana, as in 1856, but in this season the troupe also carried into Kentucky and down the Mississippi. The circus property was left near Natchez, Mississippi, over the winter, and in the spring of 1858 the route was resumed through Louisiana, Arkansas, and Texas. By December they were in Galveston, where they hired a steamboat to carry them to Mobile, Alabama.

Buckley ranged far and wide, and the reason for this is not clear, unless one accepts that he was looking for new territory. In 1859 he crossed southern Alabama, Georgia, and South Carolina, playing in many small towns, more than thirty of which are no longer on

All that was on the bills could be seen under the Buckley pavilion, as the big top was then termed. Major circus artistes were as well known in their own day as the media stars of our time. Newspaper advertisement, 1857, Circus World Museum.

the maps. They visited Florida in October and at Warrington boarded a steamer that took them to Apalachicola, New Port, Tampa, and Key West. At year's end they were in Nassau, from which they went to Haiti and Jamaica. On March 31, 1860, Buckley decided to end the sojourn, and they returned to Delavan, from which they had left in 1858.

After less than a month's rest the Great Buckley Show, as it was then titled, took to the road again, but it was a much reduced route they followed, being limited to what we now call the Midwest. "The largest, most popular, best and cheapest" was the advertising slogan. It does not appear to have been any of those things, but traveling show advertising has never been held strictly to the truth. After two performances in Goshen, Indiana, on October 25, 1860, Harry Buckley disbanded the troupe. He had five years of successful proprietorship. It would be 1874 before he organized another circus. He had the sideshow privilege with the Mabies from 1861 to 1863 and was idle, as far as can be determined, until he supplied William Coup and Dan Castello with the wagons and horses for their 1870 circus. These same chattels he sold to the P. T. Barnum circus for 1871. In 1872 and 1873 he managed the concert privilege for Barnum.

The Hippodrome movement was a phenomenon of the 1850s and an outgrowth of Victor Franconi's show in Paris in 1845. Instead of a circus ring, the hippodrome featured an oval track on which a myriad of races were held. These matched horses, ostriches, elephants, monkey-ridden ponies, and other types of mobility. The idea seems to have been to give the public something more than the traditional circus acts, which hadn't changed to any extent since the birth of the genre in the 1770s. The hippodromes didn't supplant the circus acts; they simply supplemented them with the excitement of racing.

In America, Franconi's Hippodrome of 1853 and 1854 was the first such exhibition. It was copied by Rufus Welch in 1853, and the name hippodrome (from the track surrounding the circus ring) was attached to several circus titles, most of which had no races but tried to capitalize on the name. Apparently feeling that he had carried the circus form as far as he could with his 1873 "Greatest Show on Earth," P. T. Barnum in 1874 framed what was called P. T. Barnum's Great Roman Hippodrome, a very large, well-advertised venture of a semipermanent nature in New York City.

Harry Buckley decided to copy Barnum in that 1874 season with a traveling show he titled Roman Hippodrome and Universal Fair. It was a huge company; the expenses were said to be $2,000 a day, and it was a huge failure. Circus historian William Slout has written of it, "The Buckley hippodrome show allegedly went out this year with three railroad trains, 800 men, women, children, and horses, 150 male and female champions of the Olympiad, $50,000 in Roman and Grecian chariots, $150,000 in domestic and imported thoroughbred race horses, $20,000 in racing elephants and camels, $20,000 in wardrobe, $150,000 in a free exhibit of living wild animals, and a daily expense of $3,000. Such were the Barnum-like claims,

Unusually large for a circus rider at over six feet tall and 200 pounds, Harry Buckley reportedly established the first cheese factory in Wisconsin with fellow Delavanite W. C. Coup. Photograph, undated, courtesy Gordon Yadon.

much of which, Barnum-like, was an advertising exaggeration." Along with the exaggerations was the use of the phrase "Barnum's Great New York Prototype Hippodrome," which did not sit well with Barnum and his partners and was discontinued in August after they objected. It is not known how much was lost in the failure of the Buckley version. The company finished a full season on the road and went into Cincinnati, where one Byron V. Rose took over its management.

Buckley seems to have sat out at least a year after the Hippodrome bust. The *New York Clipper* refers to an 1876 circus titled Mabie & Buckley, but which Buckley, if any, it included isn't known, and the Mabie brothers were dead by then. Harry opened a livery stable in Delavan, perhaps as early as 1870, and it was a successful operation. In 1877 he had the menagerie on the Dan Rice Circus and was manager of the company in 1878. This was his last circus employment. He left Delavan in 1882. Highly thought of in his adopted village, Buckley was a true pioneer of the Wisconsin circus. He contributed not only to Delavan's cultural scene, but also to its commercial growth, with a livery stable, a hardware store, and a cheese factory.

Coexistent with Harry Buckley in the Delavan circus circle was John Holland (1815–1887). An Englishman and an acrobat, he came to this country in 1847. That winter he introduced the Holland Family of three acrobats, which was the name he used for over twen-

The greatest flop that originated in Delavan was Harry Buckley's World's Race Festival. Playing on the fame of the Barnum Hippodrome title, the flashy bill stands and many features of the show simply did not attract sufficient patrons to make it a success. Cabinet photograph, 1874, Circus World Museum.

ty years. Their first New York engagement was at the Chatham Theatre. Nathan Howes hired them for the opening stand of his circus in Brooklyn in March and April of 1848 and sent them to the Mabies for the summer tour. It was in that winter that the Hollands took up residence in Delavan. Edmund Mabie sold John Holland 120 acres, which was his home for the rest of his life.

Holland had developed what is now known as a "barrel act" in which he stood on a barrel and moved it about the ring with his feet while one boy balanced on his shoulders and another rode inside the barrel. This scene was enhanced by the comic possibilities of the little boy inside the barrel becoming disoriented by the constant movement. John used the name Lucien, the shoulder-riding boy was Julien, and the six-year-old in the barrel was Albert. These boys were apprentices; John's oldest son wasn't born until 1850. The Holland Family was with the Mabie troupe through 1851. In 1853 and 1854 they were with the L. G. Butler Circus of Chicago. George F. Holland, at four years old, was with Butler, as was the apprentice Albert. They joined Buckley's 1856 circus, having served beside him on both the Mabie and Butler shows.

As did so many performers at one time or another, John Holland wished to be a proprietor, but as with most athletes he lacked the business acumen to organize and manage a firm, so he allied himself with a man named J. E. Mosher. As Dan Castello, another performer who later became a show owner, once said, "There has to be a practical man with every circus." Holland & Mosher's Great American Circus and Theatre opened in Delavan on May 3, 1857. More a variety show than a circus, it lasted but four months. In Holland's obituary in the *Delavan Enterprise* in 1887 is this telling statement:

> Mr. Holland was an honest man and thought everybody else the same, but he learned to his pecuniary sorrow that all men were not composed of such materials as entered into the formation of himself.

The Holland Family (now consisting of John, George, John Jr., and daughter Mary Ann) returned to the Buckley fold from 1858 through 1860. Mary Ann was a dancer and rider, George was a rider, John Jr. was a juggler, and all of them were in the family acrobatic act. Edward joined the family on tour in 1860 at age seven.

The Hollands were featured on George W. DeHaven's circus in 1861 and 1862 and B. R. Maginley's show in 1863. The family owned the Holland & Madden Circus in 1865 and then served successively with Mike Lipman, Maginley & Carroll, C. T. Ames, and P. A. Older. The last year of the family act was 1872, when they were with Ed Backenstoe's troupe. John Sr. then retired to his farm in Delavan. For fifty years he trouped in Europe and America, and his lasting gift to popular culture was the family of riders and acrobats he founded, the last of whom died in Delavan in 1960.

In Mary Ann Holland (1847–1895) we have one of the earliest circus women whose life we know beyond the confines of newspaper advertisements. Most of society held the circus in low regard (as it did the theatre and horse racing), and its participants were thought to be outside the pale, especially the women. At a time when women's roles in society were strictly defined and their deportment closely observed, circus women traveled about the country wearing skimpy costumes and facial makeup and disporting on the backs of horses or throwing themselves into acrobatic positions no proper woman would countenance. For this reason most of the female performers were the wives, sisters, or daughters of the male members of the various troupes.

Mary Ann was born in Hamburg, Germany, just before her parents came to America. She was supposedly introduced into the ring at four years of age, though she is not mentioned in notices until 1858 on the Buckley circus. In that same year her little brothers, George F. and John Jr., made their debuts. Trained as were all circus children in acrobatics and riding, the three, with their parents, engaged as what was always billed as "The Holland Family." Mary Ann was sixteen when she married George Madden (1836–1897) in 1863. He was a magician and clown who was more of a concert performer than a circus ring figure. After their marriage, Mary Ann devoted herself to concert work, being a Punch and Judy operator. She may not have performed at all after the 1865 birth of their daughter. Madden owned a dog that could speak several words, according to puppeteer David Lano, and also had a taste for whiskey. In 1861 he was his father-in-law's partner in the Holland & Madden Circus. The Maddens toured with such shows as P. A. Older, Burr Robbins, and Cooper & Bailey. Their daughter, Nora, married Joseph McMahon, proprietor of a circus that often changed its name because of the "grift," a circus word for the gambling and shortchanging that was endemic on some shows. The Maddens were on McMahon's circus from 1885 to 1894, nine years that must have been trying for Mary Ann. Gordon Yadon has written that she "could not possibly have experienced pleasant years on these shows, and spent most of her time taking care of her two young grandsons who traveled with the McMahon circus." Mary Ann Holland Madden died in Delavan on October 31, 1895, just forty-eight years old.

George F. Holland (1850–1917) was quite possibly the best rider to come out of Wisconsin. Such things are difficult to assess in retrospect, but there is no one whose record of accomplishment in the ring stands out as his does. First as an acrobat and then as a rider, he participated in the Holland Family act until August 1872. In that month George went to Chicago and joined the Chiarini circus, and in November he married Katherine Holloway. She had been apprenticed as a girl to Giuseppe Chiarini, the globe-trotting proprietor of a famous show. The two performed together until they retired in 1910. George did a principal act, including somersault riding, and Katherine was a manège (i.e., saddle) rider. To list their affiliations over the years would consume several pages. Suffice it to say that they worked for all the largest circuses of their time, titles such as Dan Rice, Burr Robbins, John Robinson (eleven seasons), Sells–Floto, and many more.

George Holland twice entered into circus partnerships. In 1885 he and his brother Edward along with John and Charles McMahon formed the Holland–McMahon Circus. The firm was a railroad circus until they reached Cincinnati, where they chartered a steamboat, the

Mountain Girl, at $100 a week with the intention of performing on the Ohio and Mississippi rivers. They played Aurora, Indiana, on November 5 and were on their way downriver, intending to appear in Rising Sun, Indiana, the next day. At about 2 a.m. the *Mountain Girl* collided with an upbound ore packet. Within minutes the circus boat sank, taking with it two workmen and all the horses, animals, and equipment. Only the tent was salvaged. The circus was valued at $20,000 and recovered $12,000 in a suit against the *Mountain Girl*'s owners. Undaunted by this calamity, George and his partners went back to Delavan and reorganized for the 1886 season. Holland, apparently dismayed at the amount of grift on the show, resigned in the spring of 1888.

In 1888 George, Edward, and the Gormley brothers, Frank and Everett, Delavanites all, framed the seven-car Holland & Gormley Allied Railroad Circus, which they toured for two years. George sold his interest in October 1889.

George and Katherine retired in 1895, for the first time, and built a hotel in Delavan. They had eleven children, and some of them, the boys, wanted to become circus riders, so George began teaching them in 1896. Once they were competent to appear before the public, they formed a new Holland Family act and went out with the John Robinson Circus in 1897. In subsequent years the family appeared at fairs, with an occasional season on circuses. George and Katherine spent their last season of performance on Sells–Floto in 1910. They lived out their remaining years in Delavan.

Edward Holland (1853–1939), his parents' second son, was also a lifelong resident of Delavan. Not as accomplished as his older brother in the ring, he enjoyed a longer circus career. He was an acrobat and rider and later worked in management at several levels. He first appeared on the Holland & Mosher Circus in 1857, at the age of four. With the Holland Family act through 1872, when John Sr. retired, Edward accompanied George to the Chiarini circus and to New Zealand and Australia. For the next ten years he was mainly with John Robinson, first as a gymnast and from 1882 to 1885 as equestrian director. He then went into business for himself, becoming a partner in the Holland–McMahon, Holland–Gormley, Holland, Bowman & McLaughlin, and the Van Amburgh shows. In 1892 he launched the E. G. Holland & Co. Railroad Circus, which in 1894 was the last circus to go out of Delavan, closing the ring on a forty-seven-year cycle. Edward became a law officer and served as the village's first chief of police from 1897 to 1903. After three more years as a circus agent (Mighty Haag and John Robinson), he accepted the managership of the New York Hippodrome and left Delavan in the fall of 1908. He died in New Jersey after a seventy-seven-year career in the circus business, surely one of the longest such records.

John Holland Jr., the last of his father's sons, was dead at twenty (story not known). He was a member of the Holland Family, as were his siblings, until the retirement of his father. In 1874 he and his brother Edward were a trapeze duo on the John Robinson circus.

We described George F. Holland as possibly the best rider to come out of Wisconsin, yet his son George E. Holland (1875–1960) may have exceeded him, or at least been a close second. Comparisons are difficult; suffice it to say that both father and son were truly outstanding practitioners of the riding art. George E. threw his first somersault on horseback when he was thirteen. He debuted before the public at fourteen, on the elder George's Holland–Gormley Circus. The next year, 1890, he was a featured principal rider on the John Robinson show. His parents left Robinson in 1893, but young George remained with the troupe through 1897. The Gollmar brothers of Baraboo enticed him away for two seasons, and he went back to Robinson in 1900. He was advertised as "The World's Greatest Somersaulting Rider," once turning fifty-six consecutive somersaults. James Robinson, the outstanding rider of a generation earlier, called him "the top equestrian on the American circus scene."

George E. married in 1901; his wife was as accomplished on the distaff side of riding as he was on the male. She was Rose Dockrill (1875–1966), daughter of Elise Dockrill, perhaps the outstanding manège rider of the day. Her father was Richard Dockrill, for many years the equestrian director on the Barnum & Bailey Circus. Educated at a Catholic school in Fordham, New York City, she learned riding under her mother's tutelage at the Barnum & Bailey winter quarters in Bridgeport, Connecticut. At seventeen she was riding for the show. In 1896 she joined the Ringling Brothers Circus, and subsequently the Walter L. Main Circus and the Adam Forepaugh & Sells Brothers Show. She met George when she joined the John Robinson company in 1901. They were married that November in Savannah, Georgia.

George E. and Rose performed as individuals and as a team. They were announced as "Holland and Dockrill, the World's Greatest Riders" and appeared on snow-white horses, of which they owned several. When George's uncle Edward Holland was equestrian manager of the New York Hippodrome, from 1908 to 1919, he saw to it that George and Rose were presented in that huge hall. George has been quoted as saying that the team's biggest thrill was performing at the Hippodrome. With casts of 500, before audiences that could reach 5,000, they had long engagements. They would open with a fast jockey act, probably because it was a rigorous turn and needed to be presented while the two were fresh. Rose did her *haute école* presentation, a demonstration of expert

Delavanites George E. and Rose Dockrill Holland were renowned for their outstanding riding acts. Here they are posed in elegant wardrobe typical of the style used by riders after the turn of the century. Photograph, undated, Rose Dockrill Holland Gift, Circus World Museum.

riding maneuvers on horseback. A carrying act, in which George stood on the horse and lifted Rose to his shoulders, and then George's always popular somersaulting routines. Gordon Yadon has written that their act never failed to bring on thunderous applause and an extra curtain call.

There was more money, and less traveling, in vaudeville than in the circus, and the Hollands availed themselves of that genre in the 1920s. Because of financial difficulties they continued to perform in their fifties. No longer headliners, they worked for small circuses. Their final public performance was on the 1938 St. Louis Police Circus. They were both 63 by then. Childless, the couple were the last of the long Holland line of circus celebrities, a chain of 100 years of ring appearances.

These families, then—the Mabies, the Buckleys, and the Hollands—were the most famous of the Delavan circus colony. But many more also played a part in the village's circus history, and therefore in Wisconsin's circus heritage. Of the professionals there was Luke Tilden, who began his career as a canvasman with the Mabies and rose to become assistant manager of the P. T. Barnum Circus. William C. Coup, who we will discuss later on in this book, came to Delavan in 1854 as a sideshow operator. Stewart Craven, menagerie supervisor for the Mabies and one of the most highly regarded elephant handlers of all time, moved to the village in 1859.

Joseph B. McMahon, whose circuses set records for "grift," that is, cheating, shortchanging, and operating crooked games, went out of Delavan for nineteen years beginning in 1888. He moved to Delavan because his brother, John, was a partner in the 1885 Holland–McMahon Circus, and Joe became an employee. After the Ohio River collision of the *Mountain Girl*, related previously, Joe McMahon took over management of the show, and as Gordon Yadon wrote, "He hired uncouth men with bad reputations, brought in all sorts of gamblers, and tolerated other unethical practices." When the circus left Delavan in the spring, as a railroad circus, it became apparent to George F. and Edward Holland that they couldn't live with the situation, so they sold out to Joe McMahon.

The Gormley brothers, Frank and Everett, natives of the village, had the Holland–Gormley Railroad Circus in 1888–1889. They also traveled with other shows, such as Burr Robbins, French & Monroe, and Rentz and Ashley.

Perhaps the involvement of nonprofessional Delavanites in the circus business is more telling of the attraction the institution held for the general public. Most of them were investors, the glimmer of great profits causing them to back their professional neighbors for a season's tour. Stephen S. Babcock, nominally a grocer, was coproprietor of the 1857 Buckley & Co. Circus. In 1870 he took a job as general agent of the Dan Castello–William C. Coup show. Greenleaf Collins, a hotel operator, had his own circus on tour in 1876. Another grocer, James Sturtevant, became fascinated with the showman's life and joined Edward Holland in framing the Van Amburgh Circus in 1891. D. Bennett Barnes, an attorney, settled in the town in 1855 and arranged financing for several circuses over the years. Eugene B. Hollister, whose resort

The large male Asiatic elephant Albert, a feature of the 1889 Holland & Gormley show, mashed the mud as he ambled past the Episcopal church in Delavan. Despite it being a scene frequently encountered in the circus center, a small contingent of street urchins excitedly accompanied the beast on his stroll around town. Photograph, 1889, courtesy Gordon Yadon.

on Lake Delavan was a popular hangout with circus people, had concessions with various shows, including those of Harry Buckley and Dan Castello. An example of Delavan's participation in the national circus scene is found in the 1871 P. T. Barnum Circus, which had thirteen villagers on its roster.

These involvements by locals were by no means unusual in circus history, nor were they confined to Delavan. All the well-known winter quarters towns—Baraboo, Janesville, and Evansville in Wisconsin and others such as Bridgeport, Connecticut, and Peru, Indiana—saw such partaking. One reason for it was that showmen seeking capital investment would call on the more successful local businessmen. And just as lawyers and doctors in Manhattan today are willing to invest in Broadway musicals, the grocers and hoteliers we have mentioned in Delavan welcomed a chance to have a piece of whatever glamour there might be in the business of traveling shows.

Had it not been for the foresight of the Mabie brothers in selecting Delavan as their permanent base, the history of the village would have been much different. It would also have been less exciting, and probably few people in Wisconsin or outside the state would have heard much of the place. After 1894, when the last Delavan circus went on the road, the village reverted to an ordinary rural town, much like any other. What it had, and has today, was the memory of itself as the circus center of Wisconsin.

HIRAM ORTON

W e are not privy to the thoughts of showmen planning shows; thus it is with some wonder that we relate the method by which Hiram Orton organized his. There are no records available; the source of our knowledge is family tradition. And since his family was a fecund lot, one hears from all sides the tale of this sailor who began the longest involvement in the circus by a single American family. The name Orton was first in a circus title in 1854, and one member of the family, noted elephant trainer William "Buckles" Woodcock, Jr., is still in the ring at this writing.

Hiram Orton (1811–1884) was born in Erie County, Pennsylvania, and became a sailor on the Great Lakes at sixteen. In 1843 he acquired a tavern in LaPorte County, Indiana. Since the lakes freeze over in winter, it is not unusual for sailors to have another source of income in those months. After ten years in Indiana, Orton moved his family to a farm near Portage City (now Portage), Wisconsin.

In the early winter of 1853, on his last voyage before the shipping season closed, he sailed from Milwaukee to Chicago. In the city he attended a circus, most likely that of L. G. Butler & Co., which played Chicago on November 10 and 11. It is said that in observing the performance, Hiram became convinced that his children could do as well as the acrobats he was watching, and that he resolved to start his own circus. This traditional version has a rather thin cover, as the acrobats with the Butler troupe were the famed Holland Family act from Delavan, but it is what has been handed down.

Orton approached two of the performers, J. A. Gilkinson and Charles Tubbs, and proposed that they spend the winter in Portage framing a circus and teaching his children to act in it. The presence of these two men with the Orton Circus in January 1854 is the first confirmed fact in this tale thus far.

Hiram's children were Miles, fifteen years old; Dennis, thirteen; Hattie, eleven; and Lester, seven. Three others were all too young to participate in this first season. By January, Tubbs and Gilkinson had taught the young Ortons enough so that they could appear in public. The father arranged for a heated amphitheater across from the Washington House hotel in Portage, and nightly performances began. The cast was the four children; Tubbs as strongman; Gilkinson as clown; Julian Harvey, a contortionist; and the seven-piece Hunt's New York Brass and String Band. Advertised as H. Orton's Circus in Portage City, the title was changed to Orton's Badger Circus when they went on the road in May. It was the first show to refer to the native state in its name.

When he abandoned the decks of Great Lakes boats to launch his family into the circus business in 1854, Hiram Orton never knew that he was commencing a 145-year association with the outdoor show industry that continues today. Photograph, undated, Circus World Museum.

Managers Gilkinson and Tubbs didn't hesitate to pursue a heavy schedule with the circus, despite the fact that half its performers were in their first year before the public. They traveled for two months in Wisconsin, two in Iowa, and two in Illinois. In November, instead of returning to Portage, they went into the South and did not return until the following June. Their route led down the Mississippi to Natchez and Vicksburg, then east through Mississippi to Alabama, and up through Tennessee and Kentucky to the Midwest.

By March 1855 they had added Henry Gardner, a clown; R. S. Kennedy, a two- and four-horse rider; Joe Tinkham, a contortionist; and several acrobats and had changed to a new band. By this time, sixteen-year-old Miles Orton was performing as a bareback rider; he would become one of the leading riders in the West in that specialty. J. E. Weeks was the advance agent and would continue for several years to see to the advertising and hotel accommodations for Orton.

This image may be a youthful representation of Miles Orton, one of the best riders in the nineteenth-century American circus. Some claim that he was the first rider to hold two people aloft while the horse galloped at full speed around the ring. Card photograph, c. 1865, E. C. May Papers, Circus World Museum.

As in 1854, the troupe made a southern excursion in the fall and winter of 1855. This time, however, instead of turning east from the Mississippi, they turned west into Louisiana, then north into Arkansas, Missouri, and Kansas. Orton's was the first circus to perform in Kansas City, which they did on April 26, 1856. Miles Orton was the principal rider, his brother Dennis did a perch act, Hattie Orton was a rider, and Washington Chambers contributed a scenic riding act.

A look at nineteenth-century morality is given to us in an incident that occurred in Arkansas. Bad roads delayed the heavy wagons on one occasion, according to the *Cincinnati Daily Commercial*. The circus set up in an open field, *sans* tent or seats. A hat was passed, and all but five of the spectators paid admission. During the performance the canvas wagon arrived, and the tent was erected. With this accomplished, the five people who had not paid then did so.

On another occasion the circus had to operate with no top to their tent for ten days, with a foot of snow on the ground. Both of these events add fuel to the notion that the public was anxious to be entertained, though no less anxious than the showmen were to sell tickets.

The company was back in Portage City in July 1856, where they took a ten-day recess before touring the northern reaches of the settled area of Wisconsin. At that time the population of the state lay south of a line from La Crosse to Green Bay, roughly analogous to the tree line, the southern edge of the vast forest covering the northern part of the state. In September, Orton reorganized at Portage for the annual southern tour.

We remarked previously that sixty percent of the early circuses performed year-round. In the summer they toured in the North, and in the fall and winter in the South. There were several differences in performing in the two areas. While a small show, such as Orton's Badger Circus, did not require as much reduction in personnel and equipment as did the larger outfits, all of them made some adjustments. Because of the generally bad roads in the southern and western states, most companies took only dead-axle wagons into those areas. These are wagons in which the axles attached to the body instead of to springs. They were easier to extract from the mudholes and swollen streams that constantly greeted them. Since the towns were smaller, the showmen could use smaller tents and fewer seats, thus lightening the weight of their shows. And, especially in the western states (Arkansas, Missouri, and so on), the circus carried extra horses—some as replacements, for those were not easy to find, and some for trading purposes.

The 1856–1857 winter tour of the Badger Circus is one of the few well-documented excursions of any nineteenth-century American circus because of a reminiscence and diary kept by Josiah May, ringmaster and agent of the company. Staff members included Hiram Orton, proprietor; John Peer, manager (later replaced); J. E. Weeks, treasurer (later manager); Tyle Orton; and May. There were four riders, Miles Orton, Den Orton, George Beatty, and R. S. Kennedy. The clowns were George Constable and Isaac Huyk. The acrobats were Joe Tinkham and Dan Kipp. Charles Tubbs was the strongman, and Billy Bird contributed an unsupported ladder act. In addition to these there were twenty-five to thirty workmen.

During the course of the tour other performers were hired and others left. Circus rosters were by no means stable. As in any business, disagreements, injuries, and offers of better pay elsewhere made the organizations impermanent in any one form. Just as they traded or bought horses as they traveled, the showmen hired and fired performers and workmen alike.

An equipment list, one of the few early ones, has come down to us, and it illustrates what it took in the way of property for a medium-sized circus to travel through the South in 1856. The tent was a 100-foot "round," that is, it was 100 feet in diameter. It had a single center pole, which stood in the middle of the 40-foot ring. The seats occupied half the circumference of the ring, and the two animal cages were along the outer wall of the tent, opposite the seats. There was as well a "dressing room canvas," a smaller tent.

Trained when seventeen years of age as a performer, Miles Orton eventually operated the largest circus ever owned by an Orton, a 24-car rail show in 1884. Family members traveled their shows overland by both wagons and motor trucks, on inland river steamboats, and by rail. Photograph, undated, Circus World Museum.

There were eight baggage wagons, two cages, a bandwagon, a carryall (for the performers), and two buggies. Twenty-two baggage horses and fourteen other horses made up the stable. Twelve of the horses pulled the bandwagon in the parades. The riders supplied their own ring horses. One cage held two lions, the other an anteater, monkeys, and a raccoon. In addition, Charles Tubbs owned a leopard, which performed in an open ring and had its own cage.

Leaving Portage, the troupe traveled through Illinois to St. Louis, then through Missouri and Arkansas, and into Louisiana. They were in Shreveport on January 2, 1857. Crossing the Mississippi at Natchez they went on to Alabama, where they spent six weeks. After a similar time in Georgia, they moved into Tennessee and Kentucky. Illinois and Wisconsin followed, and they were back in Portage on November 10. Fourteen months on the road, in all weathers, playing in cities, in villages, and at crossroads, took its toll on man, beast, and wagon. "Orton's Great Southern Circus" was sold in Portage on November 18.

There is no record as to why the sale was made. The purchasers were G. Tyle Orton, Hiram's cousin, who had joined as agent in Natchez; J. E. Weeks, the manager; Josiah May, the agent; and Charles Tubbs, the long-time employee. These gentlemen paid $10,852 for the circus, which seems to be a very high amount for the property. However, there also seems to be a hidden scenario, as Hiram Orton and P. A. Older were partners in 1858, using this self-same equipment.

The four purchasers, Orton, Weeks, Tubbs, and May, were employees of this new-old concern, which traveled under the name of Orton & Older's Great Southern Circus. Older, it will be remembered, had sold his interest in the Mabie circus in 1854. This was announced in some ads as follows:

> Mr. Orton would state to the former patrons of his exhibition that he has disposed of a half interest in this popular concern to Mr. P. A. Older, formerly of the firm of Mabie, Older & Co.

Opening day was May 9 in Portage City. The circus went into Iowa and Missouri, as was their custom, but then veered east into Illinois, Kentucky, and Tennessee. The Deep South was next, and they went into Alabama and Georgia.

Disaster struck on the night of November 17 in Montgomery, Alabama. The livery stable in which the horses were boarded caught fire. Some of the animals escaped, but in running loose several were stolen. Older bought all the horses and harness available in the town but had to hire teams to haul the show for some time. The tent was pitched across the street from the stable and flying sparks had burned up the top of it, so the circus was presented in a side-walled arrangement for two weeks.

On November 25 in Auburn, Alabama, the entire roster was arrested on suspicion of murder. There had been a fight in Lockapoko, and a store-

Josiah M. "Si" May was the ringmaster and general stock agent for the Orton circus in the late 1850s. Like a few other show people, he maintained a diary in which he entered the routes of the Orton circus for five years. Diary, 1856–1860, E. C. May Papers, Circus World Museum.

keeper was stabbed to death. As it turned out, a local blacksmith was the killer; no circus people were involved. However, the show people were detained for eleven days and lost eight days' receipts (about $8,000).

Historically, the Orton & Older troupe is important for presenting one of the first after-show concerts. These were in the nature of olios, presenting songs, dances, and the like. Orton & Older's was a minstrel show given in the main tent following the circus program. Patrons paid twenty-five cents to see "burlesques, song and dance, comicalities, etc." These became common in the years before the Civil War and were still offered as late as the mid-twentieth century. It was a way in which a few more coins could be coaxed out of persons already seated in the tent.

From Alabama in December 1858, the company moved north along the coast as far as Alexandria, Virginia, and returned to Alabama in July. One gets the impression that the managers were trying to find a paying route, but could not. The Panic of 1857 was still affecting the economy. In August the circus headed west, crossing Mississippi and Arkansas, and arrived in Texas on September 28, 1859. Here they wandered for four months before again going east into Louisiana and Alabama.

The heiress to a famous circus name, Mary Ann Cooke Cole, joined the company in late May 1860. Divorced from William Cole, she was trying to continue her career alone. Her ability as a manège rider was above the average, but not so good that she could hire on to one of the larger eastern circuses. The Cooke

The earliest surviving contract for the sale of a Wisconsin circus covers the transfer of the Hiram Orton circus. Seventy-two percent of the $10,852 price of the circus was in its ring and baggage horses. Manuscript, 1857, E. C. May Papers, Circus World Museum.

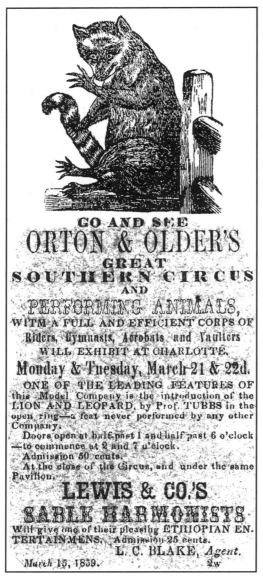

GO AND SEE
ORTON & OLDER'S
GREAT
SOUTHERN CIRCUS
AND
PERFORMING ANIMALS,
WITH A FULL AND EFFICIENT CORPS OF
Riders, Gymnasts, Acrobats and Vaulters
WILL EXHIBIT AT CHARLOTTE,
Monday & Tuesday, March 21 & 22d.
ONE OF THE LEADING FEATURES OF
this Model Company is the introduction of the
LION AND LEOPARD, by Prof. TUBBS in the
open ring—a feat never performed by any other
Company.
Doors open at half past 1 and half past 6 o'clock
—to commence at 2 and 7 o'clock.
Admission 50 cents.
At the close of the Circus, and under the same
Pavilion,
LEWIS & CO.'S
SABLE HARMONISTS
Will give one of their pleasing ETHIOPIAN EN-
TERTAINMENS. Admission 25 cents.
L. C. BLAKE, *Agent.*
March 15, 1859. 2w

*Another of P. A. Older's associations with
Wisconsin's circus impresarios was a
partnership with Hiram Orton 1858–1860.
The novelty of a lion and leopard uncaged
in the ring, along with the minstrel concert,
augmented the largely ground-based acts of
the circus. Newspaper advertisement, 1859,
Circus World Museum.*

family, well-known in England, had performed in America in 1836 and 1837 and then returned to England. Mary Ann and her husband had stayed in this country when the family left.

Obviously in some straits, Older began advertising the company as Cooke's Royal Circus in June and alternated the two titles over the rest of the season. This attempt did little to revive prospects. A swing through Minnesota and Wisconsin ended at Rockford, Illinois, on September 15, 1860. The record doesn't say how much salaries were in arrears at the closing, but that they were is fact.

Thus Hiram Orton's managerial career came to an end. Son Miles Orton revived the name beginning in 1864, but by then the family was living in Iowa. Hiram Orton served in some capacity with several of the subsequent Orton circuses, but never again as the owner. A sailor who thought his children were as good as the acrobats he saw in 1853 in Chicago was vindicated when they and their children, and their children's children, persevered in circus management until 1932.

DAN CASTELLO

One of the best-known names in Wisconsin circus history is that of Dan Castello (1832–1909). He was an owner, a partner, and a performer in a host of troupes, and he had his name in the title of most of them. Other showmen considered his name to be so valuable that it appeared in the title of circuses of which he owned no part. He was with companies in Delavan, Fairplay, and Racine, spreading himself across the map of Wisconsin. Though he is not known for it, that is, no account of his career has mentioned it, he was a prime mover in the adoption of railroad travel by circuses. And his circuses possibly traveled more widely by railroad than any other of his day.

Born in Kingston, Ontario, in 1832, Castello may have begun his circus career in 1849. An article in the New York *Mercury* in 1873 uses this date and says he was an apprentice with the June & Turner Circus of Danbury, Connecticut. George Holland dates Castello's arrival in Delavan as 1854, when he joined the Mabie circus as an acrobat, but nothing in the Mabie records affirms this. His initial appearance in advertising was as a clown with the John Robinson Circus in 1856. An unusually reticent man for a public figure, his early biography is difficult to follow.

Castello's wife, Frances, first appears with him in the notices in 1857. She was eventually an accomplished rider. They were with Harry Buckley in 1857 as well as serving with Major Brown's Colosseum. That winter, Dan went alone to New Orleans with Spalding & Rogers. Eighteen-fifty-eight was spent with Satterlee, Bell & Co.

Confined to western shows to this point, Castello, who worked as both clown and acrobat, trained a bull that he named Don Juan and with it went east to join James Nixon's company. It was the first contact between two very active nineteenth-century showmen. During the season he purchased a trained buffalo from George Goodwin in Boston. In October 1859 he journeyed with the bull and the buffalo to England, where he appeared with Hengler's circus and later with Howes & Cushing's American Circus. His leaping act was much appreciated in England, to the point that Charles Dickens, an inveterate circusgoer, mentioned him in a pamphlet thusly: "Young Castello did not jump, he flew." He consistently leaped a dozen horses from the low springboard. Pierre Couderc credited him as one of the few acrobats to accomplish a triple somersault.

An injury put an end to the English sojourn, and Castello returned to America in October 1860, after just one year. That winter he was again with Spalding & Rogers, this time in New York at the Bowery Theatre. A few of the company were sent to New Orleans in January 1861 to perform aboard the famous circus barge, the *Floating Palace*. Pete Conklin, the clown, was among them, and we have his version of events following the Louisiana secession:

One of the truly great circus men of the nineteenth century, Dan Castello's accomplishments and contributions are just beginning to be appreciated. For over fifty years he did it all, from personally performing in the ring to training animals, managing shows and owning them. Tintype, undated, Circus World Museum.

Dan Castello

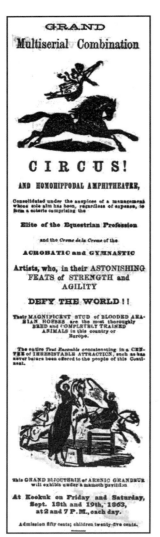

Exclamations and adjectives, along with highly inventive titles, characterized circus advertisements by the time of the Civil War. Filling an entire column of a newspaper and including several cuts, the circus ads stood out among other mundane promotions of the era. Newspaper advertisement, 1863, Circus World Museum.

The confederate government stopped our show and seized the Palace, and ordered all northern people to leave the South … We all got together and organized a company, chartered a small steamboat … and showed our way up the river … it was called Dan Castello's Great Show.

Having the show named for him indicates the respect that the performers had for Castello. It was the first time his name was in a title. The circus was short-lived, being disbanded once it reached the North. It may have been at this time that Dan and his wife moved to Racine. He is not found on any roster until August 1862, when he joined G. W. DeHaven's Union Circus in St. Louis.

A man by the name of Richard Van Valkenberg, who had made a fortune in lead mining in Fairplay, Wisconsin, like many another moneyed men decided to invest in a circus. Using the name Van Vleck, he succumbed to Dan Castello's suggestion that they form a partnership in 1863. Fairplay lies eight miles from Dubuque, Iowa, and, according to the *Dubuque Herald* at that time, "is a live, thriving village … (which has) three hotels, several blacksmith's shops, carpenters' and joiners' shops, a schoolhouse, a few saloons, and lastly (in 1863) a magnificent circus, which performs daily." After several months of appearances (actually rehearsals) in the building, the troupe went on the road in May 1863.

The firm was capitalized at $20,000, none of it Castello's. It had fifty-six horses and fifteen wagons. Isaac LaRue of Chicago built the rolling stock. The tent cost $2,600. Forty-eight workmen were hired, and ten performers, plus Castello, of course. "Castello and Van Vleck's Mammoth Circus" featured Castello and his wife, Frances; riders Joe Tinkham, William J. Smith, and John Glenroy; clown Thomas Burgess; and four acrobats. Glenroy was the best of the lot, turning somersaults on his barebacked horse. Castello clowned and presented the trained horse, Monitor, and his bull, Don Juan. The twelve-member band was under a Mr. Frehe. Glenroy wrote (in 1885) that the season was one of the most successful he ever participated in.

Stepping out of Wisconsin for a season, Castello organized a river show in Minnesota for 1864. It may well be that whoever it was that supplied the money was a resident of St. Paul—it may have been George DeHaven—as that's where the company was organized. On the other hand, river shipping was not readily available because of the war, and Castello may have had to journey to St. Paul to charter a steamboat. The one he secured was the *Jeanette Roberts*, a stern-wheeler built in 1857. Her usual work was done on the Minnesota River.

Transporting a circus by steamer had certain advantages over travel by wagon, and disadvantages as well. Since few or no wagons were carried, there could be no menagerie. Some troupes included a bandwagon, but Castello chose to mount his band on horseback. They would parade through the town on show day. The seats, tents, and properties were "gillied" to the lot, that is, they were moved by either knockdown wagons or hired drays.

Since his band was mounted, we must assume that Castello used knockdown wagons pulled by the band horses. The personnel slept and ate on the steamboat.

The advantages included not having to feed twenty or thirty horses or their teamsters, not using hotels, and not being forced to travel on bad roads. In addition, the cost of water transport was one-tenth that of overland travel.

The disadvantages, besides having to decrease the size of the troupe, were that river travel was not always dependable because of low water or fog, and there were not as many places to show on the rivers as on land. If we look at river travel as linear, bound by the riverbanks, it becomes obvious that overland travel had the greater potential for finding places to perform.

Dan Castello's Great American Circus of 1864 was apparently a partnership between Castello and George W. DeHaven. Levi J. North, the great bareback rider, was the manager. Except for Frances Castello, none of the performers were people we associate with the various Wisconsin circuses.

One of the hazards of wartime was experienced in either Terre Haute or Evansville, Indiana, when the government confiscated the boat and put the company ashore. Refitting for overland travel was expensive. The circus traveled north to Chicago and from there visited some of the Wisconsin towns. In October they played Memphis for two weeks and arranged for another steamboat, aboard which they went into Arkansas. The show was much reduced from the beginning of the season, having but twelve horses. They arranged their route to follow the advance of the Seventeenth Corps and played mainly to soldier audiences.

The wagons and horses were left in the South, and in March 1865, Dan Castello's Great Show opened in Natchez, Mississippi. DeHaven was no longer involved. The roster of performers was the strongest Castello had headed in his career. James and Josie DeMott, Carlotta DeBerg, Francoise Tourniaire, and Frances Castello were the riders. Castello advertised himself as one whose "wit, humor, conversational powers, and refinement render him the most acceptable talker who has ever entered the arena." "Worthy" may have been a better word than "acceptable," but the meaning is the same. He also presented his trained horses, Czar and Floating Cloud.

In June in Nashville, the circus acquired some equipment from Seth B. Howes, and a new partner, Egbert Howes, Seth B.'s nephew. Seth B. Howes may have bankrolled Egbert's half of the investment. The title was changed to Howes & Castello's Great Circus, and they traveled mainly in Kentucky. In Nashville again, on October 14 they mounted the show on the railroad and set off on a route through the Deep South. This was Castello's introduction to railroad transportation, a method he was to follow from then through his 1875 season with P. T. Barnum and William C. Coup. Across Georgia and Alabama, visiting only the larger towns, they came to Mobile, where they played two weeks in late November before moving on to New Orleans. The partners went up the Mississippi and in Memphis on January 6, 1866, closed out the firm.

Dan Castello

Our statement that they played only the larger towns is historically significant in that it presaged the disappearance of small towns from the routes of the larger circuses. In twenty-four days their itinerary looked like this:

Atlanta, Georgia, October 25 to 28.

Traveled on Sunday to Augusta, Georgia, October 30 to November 4.

Traveled on Sunday to Macon, Georgia, November 6 to 8.

Traveled on Thursday to Columbus, Georgia, November 10 and 11.

Traveled on Sunday to Montgomery, Alabama, played one week.

Traveled on Sunday to Mobile, Alabama, played two weeks.

The ability to bypass the smaller, and likely unprofitable, towns because of the use of the railroads was the very reason William C. Coup and P. T. Barnum decided to place that huge show on rails in 1872. That Castello was able to add to that argument through his own experience is difficult to doubt.

When Howes and Castello parted in Memphis in January 1866, James Nixon appeared on the scene and bought Howes's half of the equipment, and he and Castello, under the name Dan Castello's Great Show, opened the season in Memphis in late January. Nixon was the manager, and Castello, as usual, saw to the performance. With Nixon leading, they crossed the South as far as Virginia, then came back to St. Louis, where they played a week in April. After a run through Missouri and Iowa, they entered Wisconsin and were in Milwaukee in July. From there they went directly to Port Huron, Michigan, illustrating the speed of railroad transport by accomplishing the trip on a Sunday, thus losing no performances.

Two months in Canada, going as far east as Quebec City, were followed by another trip to Georgia. This was heady stuff, moving across the settled portion of the country, from as far west as Kansas City to the East Coast twice in a single season and appearing in all the major cities. Never before had so much territory been covered by a circus. In this same season of 1866, Lewis B. Lent mounted his New York Circus on the railroads for the first time, which has been hailed by historians as a great feat, yet Lent played only New England and New York State, was on the road but four months, and went no farther west than Buffalo. The difference between the two enterprises, of course, was that Lent was an eastern showman whose progress was watched by big-city newspapers, whereas the Nixon–Castello company was out in the far reaches of the country where publicity was less available, thus their railroad accomplishment went almost unnoticed. As for Castello, his rail experience over the two seasons, 1865 and 1866, placed him at the forefront of those who moved whole circuses by train.

When we use the term "whole circuses," we mean that all the equipment, parade paraphernalia, menagerie, and personnel were thus transported. No earlier railroad circuses carried more than the basics—tent, seating, horses, and people. Many of them carried no draft animals, relying on local drayage for the move from train to lot. They were almost a mirror of the steamboat operation that we mentioned earlier.

The season ended in Mobile, Alabama, where the show spent two months at rest. They left Mobile on March 13, 1867, and by April 22 were joined by a Van Amburgh menagerie. The Van Amburgh interests had two groups of animals, one they kept to themselves and one they leased to circuses. In addition they arranged to lease a supply of oddities from P. T. Barnum's New York Museum. This gave them access to Barnum's name, which was no small favor. They operated in 1867 under the title Barnum's Museum Collection, Van Amburgh's Menagerie in connection with Dan Castello's Great Show. The season was spent in the South, Louisville, Kentucky, being the most northern stand. They ended the tour in Washington, D.C., in February 1868, when the Barnum and Van Amburgh portions reverted to their owners. The company had traveled near to 20,000 miles, averaging seventy-five miles a day.

Frederick, Maryland, was the site of the opening stand of the 1868 season. Still on the railroads but without the Van Amburgh and Barnum additions, the company used various combinations of the Nixon, Howes, and Castello names as Egbert Howes had returned as treasurer and partner. Ownership was divided—half to Castello and a quarter each to Nixon and Howes. This tour was largely in the northern tier of states. Since the railroad gauges (the distance between the rails), north and south, were different, they played on the southern gauge in 1867 and on the northern gauge in 1868. By July they had performed in Ohio, Michigan, Illinois, and Wisconsin. Their stand in Racine on June 24 may have been Castello's first professional visit to the town of his residence. They continued through Iowa, Kansas, Missouri, and into the South, wintering once again in Mobile, Alabama.

One of the great circus accomplishments fell to the lot of the Nixon, Howes, and Castello partnership in 1869. In that season they went from coast to coast, from Charleston, South Carolina, to San Francisco, California, by rail. Though it was no startling conception—after all, the railroad was there—still it was an audacious undertaking, one that linked the showmen with the great period of American expansion. Once west of Omaha, they were in new territory, experiencing the technological advances of the time with an old and proven type of entertainment.

The circus reached Omaha on the 26th of May, sixteen days after the driving of the golden spike into the ties at Promontory, Utah, that completed the transcontinental railroad. James Nixon was a passenger on the first through train to California. He wired to the circus to proceed west.

There were eleven performers in addition to Castello. Five of these were the Lowanda family of riders under Alexander Lowanda—Martinho, Clarinda, Abelardo, and Natilio. Jule Kent and Castello were the clowns. Thomas Peppers, Henry Beatty, and John Batchelor were the acrobats; William Sparks, the strongman. Frank Nash was the elephant trainer, Charles Winner the lion trainer. In addition there was the band under a Mr. Olenshaw and a minstrel troupe. Charles C. Pell was the agent, Egbert Howes the treasurer, and Nixon the manager.

The circus presented a daily street parade, featuring a new Fielding-made bandwagon from the Van Amburgh company, which was also the source of the lion act. Two elephants, Jenny Lind and a calf, Hop-O-My-Thumb; ten cages of animals; and two camels composed the menagerie. The physical property was transported on eight cars, and the personnel rode in passenger service.

Their tour was one of the most successful in circus history. Crowded houses greeted them at every stop, for they were often the first circus of any size to appear in those reaches. Full houses were reported in Omaha and Cheyenne. To reach Denver, to which the railroad did not extend, the show went overland from Cheyenne, 101 miles to the south. "We have never seen the streets of Denver so crowded," said the *Rocky Mountain News*. Denver's population was less than 5,000, but six performances drew 1,200 to 1,500 people at $1.50 for adults and $1 for children.

The hike from Cheyenne to Denver proved fatal to the smaller of the two elephants. It caught pneumonia and was dead in a few days. The circus went into the gold mining towns, Golden and Central City. The latter was a wide-open town, almost lawless. In his perfunctory style Castello described it as "pretty brisk." They descended to Boulder for June 15, then back to Cheyenne and the railroad. At Laramie, Wyoming, two bandits were publicly hanged on the day the circus opened, but that did not deter people from buying tickets to see Castello leap over horses and hear his clown's patter. The Lowanda riding act received reviewers' plaudits all along the route.

In Utah, so largely Mormon, Castello paid a visit to Brigham Young, the church leader, and offered to pay to the church the same amount he had been paying the federal government as war tax. As a consequence, Young urged his flock to attend the circus, and business was excellent all through the state. The troupe crossed Nevada, playing seven dates there, and reached Truckee, California, on July 17.

For the next three months they toured in California, including a month's stand in San Francisco. The latest advertisement found was one in Redwood City for October 21. Shortly thereafter, the company returned to San Francisco, where it was sold to a trio of West Coast

Horse acts formed the basis of the circus performance since the first one in America in 1793. Here are some of Castello's equines, posed in front of what may be the show's big top after their 1869 transcontinental journey. Card stereograph, 1869, Sacramento, California, courtesy John and Mable Ringling Museum of Art, Sarasota, Florida.

showmen. Castello, Nixon, and Howes netted $120,000 on the season. In an 1899 interview Castello stated that in one 31-day period they had $1,000 a day in profits.

Returning to Racine flush with money, Castello entertained notions of retiring from the ring, according to Gordon Yadon. However, William C. Coup of Delavan approached him on the subject of starting another circus. Their discussions were to culminate in Dan Castello's Circus & Egyptian Caravan of 1870, the chattels of which were the physical basis of P. T. Barnum's Circus of 1871.

The partners mounted the show on a Great Lakes propeller, the *Benton*, with the intention of playing lake ports in Wisconsin and Michigan, a territory seldom visited by circuses. The demand for iron ore and timber during the Civil War had increased the population of the area, and towns had come into existence where there had been none ten years earlier. Because the circus would travel by water, they would have no initial investment in wagons or draft horses; thus the cost of framing the circus was not great.

Castello trained the horses in the ring barn at his home in Racine. He had his trained horses, Czar and Floating Cloud; two comic mules; and a pony for his famous "January" act. The latter, which he introduced to the circus, was as often performed with a mule as with a pony. In it the ringmaster bought the animal from the clown. When the clown left the ring, the ringmaster couldn't get the pony to move. The clown returned, whispered in the animal's ear, and it would do his bidding. There were variations in the act over the years, but the essentials are as we've indicated.

Coup had purchased eight camels from the group the army had used in the Southwest, and he added them to the show, thus the "Egyptian Caravan" in the title. Their parade through the streets of the lumber towns drew much attention. They were also used in the performance, a fact the advertising claimed was the initiation of such practice.

Coup apparently supervised the hiring of the staff and workmen, as most of them came from Delavan. George Bishop was the manager and Edward Buckley his assistant. Stephen S. Babcock was the advance agent and W. M. Gildersleeve his right-hand man. Coup also at various times helped with the advance, as attested to by newspaper accounts of his presence.

In addition to Castello, who clowned and presented his trained quadrupeds, there was Frances Castello in her manège act; an English bareback rider named George Saunders; Philo Nathans, a pad rider; Dan Castello Jr., an apprentice; and three women riders, Estelle Nathans, Frances Donaldson, and Mlle. Virginie. Muscular acts were the trapezists Miaco, Hawley, and Rivers, and the ground (or mundane) acrobats, Charles, George, and Henry Salinyea.

Erected in 1870 and serving Castello as a training enclosure for over three decades, his ring barn tied him to the Racine community. Here he trained horses with splendid names, such as "Floating Cloud" and "Czar," that later astounded audiences with their precise execution of human commands. Half-tone, circa 1902, Circus World Museum.

Castello and Coup's 1870 show served as the launching pad for the P. T. Barnum circus of 1871, the enterprise that precipitated the expansion of the circus into a great national institution. Newspaper advertisement, 1870, Circus World Museum.

The tent was erected in Racine on May 18, and rehearsals began shortly thereafter. While awaiting the arrival of the *Benton*, the troupe played two inland dates, Union Grove on May 26 and Burlington on May 27. The stand in Racine, May 28, was a sellout for both performances, as Castello was popular in his adopted hometown. The circus boarded the ship the next day and sailed to St. Joseph, Michigan. Twelve days later they crossed Lake Michigan again, to play Milwaukee. The route ahead led up the Wisconsin shore. Port Washington, Sheboygan, Manitowoc, Two Rivers, Kewanee, and Ahnepee were touched in turn. The boat went through the channel to play Sturgeon Bay, then dropped south to Green Bay and into the Fox River to DePere. Duluth and Oconto were next, and then the show moved into Michigan.

The circus did not return to Wisconsin until August 16, when they performed in Kenosha. In the meantime they had toured the Upper Peninsula of Michigan, both sides of Lake Huron as far south as Port Huron, and returned into Lake Michigan. After Kenosha they went to Waukegan and from there to Racine, where their charter ended.

Desiring to tour overland, they had made a contract with two gentlemen from Delavan, D. B. Barnes and Harry Buckley, to provide fourteen wagons and forty-two horses for the purpose. The cost of these was $3,600, and the ownership rested with Barnes and Buckley. The wagons were made by the Fish Brothers Wagon Company of Racine, a well-known firm at that time. These wagons and these horses were the physical basis of the Barnum circus of 1871.

After playing various Wisconsin towns for two months, Coup and Castello ended their season at Winona, Minnesota, on October 19. They then returned to Delavan and stored the chattels at Coup's farm. Coup has been quoted as saying, "Our trip was one of perpetual delight and not a little pecuniary profit." He valued the property at $30,000.

For the next five years, 1871 to 1875, Castello was with the Barnum show, which we will touch upon in the following chapter. He was in charge of the performance, and the arena portion of the big circus was advertised as Dan Castello's Great Show. He appeared in the ring with his marvelously trained horses, as well as acting as equestrian director. Wife Frances, son Harry, and apprentice Johnny were all riders with the company in 1871. Dan's apprentice, Dan Castello Jr., appeared three times in the program—as bareback rider, scenic rider, and clown.

At the end of the traveling season, Barnum was willing to winter the circus in Racine, perhaps at Castello's suggestion. Twelve acres west of the Chicago & Northwestern tracks at Doud Street was available at a price of $1,000 an acre. Frances Castello, however, liked her home on Lake Avenue and refused to move. Later, Castello found another parcel at 12th and Main streets but again was thwarted by his wife. Apparently, he planned to live at the quarters, leasing the place to the circus, and needed to sell his home in order to accomplish this. In any event, it was by that margin that Racine, Wisconsin, missed becoming the circus center that Bridgeport, Connecticut, later became.

Two important changes took place in the 1872 Barnum circus, and Castello was involved in both of them. The first was the mounting of this huge concern on the railroad; it was the largest circus to undertake such a project to that time. Castello, with five years' expertise at railroad movement, though admittedly with eight- to ten-car shows, was the only man to bring such experience to the sixty-car Barnum behemoth.

The second change was the expansion of the arena from one to two rings. Castello claimed later that it was his suggestion to Barnum to do this. In the one ring arena, rows of reserved-seat chairs surrounded the ring, and behind these were the tiered seats, the bleachers. People from the back rows of the bleachers had a tendency to crowd forward in the aisles to see better. They blocked the view of those in the reserved seats, who then stood on their chairs to view the ring. This blocked the sight line of those behind them. The lack of any crowd control was the major complaint of several commentators. By going to two rings, the firm solved this problem.

Castello himself was the only member of his family in the 1872 program, and George Madden, as clown, was the only Delavanite, but there was again a corps of staff members whom Coup had recruited in Delavan. Luke Tilden was assistant manager, and Henry and Edward Buckley had the cookhouse and concert privileges. George Coup, William's brother, had the candy privilege.

This was the first season in which the phrase "The Greatest Show on Earth" was used by Barnum, and it might well have been true, yet the 1873 version was even grander. Profits in 1872 were $280,000 on a million-dollar gross; in 1873 the gross was a million and a half and the profit $750,000. Castello's twenty percent must have enriched him handsomely; no division of the spoils has been reported. His apprentice, Dave Castello, appeared twice in the 1873 program, and Dan himself presented one of his trick horses. His main task was still equestrian director.

Barnum abandoned the traditional circus in 1874 and 1875. Wishing to, in his words, "do a big thing for the public and make it unobjectionable to the most refined and moral," he had Coup lease the abandoned New York & Harlem Railroad property at Fourth Avenue and Twenty-Sixth streets in New York for the conversion of the site into a huge hippodrome. The new firm was called P. T. Barnum's Great Roman Hippodrome, and the staff was largely unchanged from the 1873 Barnum circus. Dan Castello was still "Director of Amusements."

James M. Nixon, Castello's former partner and manager, was brought in as Castello's assistant in 1874, and we don't doubt that the program and races of the Hippodrome were his work. He had a great deal of experience in staging pageants, tournaments, and spectacles, whereas Castello had little. Nixon's title was "Superintendent of Amusements."

For the first time since 1871 Castello did not appear in the arena with his trick horses. The Hippodrome mixed races on the hippodrome track with circus acts, which appeared in the "infield," or overhead on trapeze and tightwire.

After three months of successful performances, in which audiences approached 20,000 a day, the Hippodrome took to the road. They visited five cities between August 3 and October 24. In order these were Boston, Philadelphia, Baltimore, Pittsburgh, and Cincinnati. On

November 2 a winter season was begun at the New York site.

The partners decided to play one-day stands in 1875. This was accomplished by having fifteen men five days ahead of the concern who constructed walls and seats that were covered by a canvas top. Two tops were alternately erected at consecutive dates in order to do this. Again, as in 1874, Castello managed but did not perform in the arena. Our guess is that James Nixon was in charge of the several tournaments and spectacles.

Coup had determined to end his connection with Barnum as early as 1874, and Castello went with him once the 1875 tour had ended. The 1875 tour was not successful, yet Castello claimed he left the partnership with $75,000 in hand. He had originally invested $60,000 in 1871.

He returned to Racine, thinking as he had in 1869 that retirement from the field was an option. He was in his forties and had spent over twenty years under canvas. But his name still held a promise, as a man named George Bushnell indicated by offering to put it once again in a circus title. Bushnell lived in Delavan and proposed to frame the largest circus ever to go out from that hive of circus activity. He had purchased a menagerie that had been on Springer's Cirkzooladon in 1875 and added to it two sea elephants leased from W. C. Coup. These monsters cost the show $1,000 a week to exhibit, and that expense had much to do with the ultimate collapse of the affair. Castello was the equestrian director, and the staff was mostly from Delavan. There is almost no information on the 1876 tour season of the Centennial Circus, which lasted from May to August.

The editor of the *Delavan Republican* took a potshot at Castello that winter by writing:

If anyone wants to lose money, just invest in Dan Castello's new circus,

which is forming in Racine and will open in the Black Hills country next spring.

He obviously blamed Castello for the failure of the Centennial Circus of the previous season. And he may have had some justification in his attitude, because it was to Castello that Coup offered the sea elephants.

Contrary to that editorial, there was no Castello circus in 1877. Castello left the circus business to spend four years mining gold in the Black Hills of the Dakota Territory. As with so many other seekers after mineral fortune, he never had a successful strike.

In 1881 he returned to the field shows, his name in the title of several failed ventures. He helped William H. Harris get the Nickel Plate show up and running in 1883 and was its equestrian director at various times over the years. He finally left Harris after the 1903 season. Castello was then seventy-one years of age, a very old man by the demographics of that day. He trained a horse act for George W. Hall in 1905, which was his last circus affiliation.

Dan Castello died in Racine on July 27, 1909. He had tasted every part of the circus of his day—the mud shows, steamboats, and rail travel. He had been performer, director, horse trainer, and circus owner. Few had greater experience, or a better reputation in the business. Barnum said of him, "Give me Dan Castello and money enough to reach the first stop, and I'll come home with a fortune at the end of the season, I don't care if it rains every day." As fine an encomium as any showman ever received.

WILLIAM CAMERON COUP

A t the completion of the first season's tour of the P. T. Barnum circus, a commentator in the *New York Clipper* wrote:

There are very few men who could have managed the Barnum show as Billy Coup has done, for, besides displaying great executive ability and a wonderful foresight, he is always the gentleman, whether dealing with a governor or a canvasman; and hereafter, when the great Barnum show is mentioned, much of its success will be attributed to its able manager, Billy Coup.

This paragraph summed up the character of William C. Coup (1836–1895) as well as any description of him ever did. For a brief period in the 1870s he was at the forefront of the entertainment business in America, and though he went on to other successes, and failures, his organization and management of the Barnum circus from 1871 to 1873, and the Barnum Hippodrome in 1874 and 1875, stands out as one of the preeminent efforts in the history of the genre.

An ongoing discussion among historians concerns who was most responsible for the success of the Barnum enterprise in its early years. Some credit Barnum while others credit Coup, which leads us to suspect that neither could have done it without the other. The combination of these two energetic gentlemen created a synergy that led the American field show in a new direction and created what has since been labeled "the Golden Age of the Circus."

William C. Coup was born to a tavern owner in Mount Pleasant, Indiana, in 1836. At twelve years old he became a printer's "devil," or helper, in the local newspaper office. In the next year he left for a larger journal in Terre Haute, Indiana. Seeing no quick reward in that business, he became a member of a traveling show. In his own words he "wanted to see something of the world." This is the most common reason given by nineteenth-century showmen for "running away to join the circus." He hired himself to P. T. Barnum's Grand Colossal Museum and Menagerie, apparently as a workman. This was not quite a circus, but rather a field show featuring attractions from Barnum's Museum in New York and a menagerie. Eight elephants brought from Ceylon was the chief animal display, there never having been so many under one ownership before that time.

The Barnum company had been on tour each year since 1851, and Coup joined it on July 11, 1853, during its stand in Terre Haute. How long he was with this caravan is not known, but in his autobiography he speaks of later being with the L. G. Butler Circus. This might have been any time between 1854 and 1856. He was with the Mabie show in 1858. His position was as the "talker" with the sideshow, the man who tried to induce the

The innovative and competent Coup managed a thousand logistical details to make a success of the unprecedented P. T. Barnum show. Unfortunately, the success he enjoyed in that partnership was never duplicated with his own circus. Photograph, undated, Richard V. Coup Gift, Circus World Museum.

public to step inside. In that year he took up residence in Delavan. In the next year he was on Harry Buckley's North American Circus, again in the sideshow. Coup married Henrietta Bradley of Kenosha in 1860; he was then twenty-four years old.

In the winter of that year he and George S. Cole of the Mabie show had a wax figure exhibition in the Caribbean. Returning to Delavan, Coup became Harry Buckley's partner in the Mabie sideshow. This lasted for the 1861 season, when Coup bought out Buckley. For the next three years Coup operated his sideshow profitably, in addition to being assistant manager of the Mabie company. In February 1865 he enlisted in the 46th Wisconsin Volunteer Infantry Regiment, was sent to Kentucky for nine months of guard duty, and then was discharged, the war being over.

From 1866 to 1869 he was a member of the Yankee Robinson Consolidated Show. He was apparently assistant manager to P. A. Older and may have had the sideshow privilege. In 1870 Coup and Castello got together to form Dan Castello's Great Circus and Egyptian Caravan, as we outlined in the preceding chapter.

To this point Coup's experience was little different from that of many showmen, or men in any business. It was a steady climb from roustabout to assistant manager. With the Castello connection he at last became a part owner. Yet even then he did not have his name in the show title. Thus, when we come to his importuning of P. T. Barnum, he does not seem to have had outstanding credentials. It must have been his reputation that caused Barnum, when asked why he agreed to become partners with an obscure western impresario, to describe him as "a capital showman, and a man of good judgment, integrity, and excellent executive ability."

A hard luck showman who never achieved lasting financial success was the story of Fayette Lodawick "Yankee" Robinson. He was among W. C. Coup's first employers and later lent his name to the fledgling Ringling enterprise in 1884. Photograph, undated, F. Beverly Kelley Gift, Circus World Museum.

Sometime in the latter half of 1870, Coup approached Barnum with the idea of using the famous showman's name on the Castello–Coup circus. Barnum demurred, citing his age and the fact that he was retired. Coup persisted, saying he wanted only his name and was willing to pay for its use. At the time Barnum received a three-percent portion of the receipts of his former museum in New York, and Coup might have projected something along those lines. Barnum, however, accepted the idea of being an active partner. "I thought I had finished the show business, but just for a flyer, I got it once more," he wrote a friend. He enthusiastically set about arranging for museum and menagerie attractions, and was especially involved in the advertising for the new venture. Coup and Barnum shared the view that the secret to successful field show operations depended on a great deal of advertising. Coup had shown this in 1870, when his "wall art," that is, his prodigious use of posters, was remarked upon by the press.

The division of ownership of P. T. Barnum's Great Traveling Museum, Menagerie, Caravan and Hippodrome was two-thirds to Barnum, and Coup and Castello splitting the remainder. Barnum had his son-in-law, S. H. Hurd, appointed as treasurer in order to protect his interest, but otherwise he left the personnel choices to Coup. This resulted in many Delavan residents on the payroll.

In addition to Coup himself as general manager and Castello as equestrian director, there were Ed Buckley, Luke Tilden, Harry Buckley, George Bushnell, William Smith, Bob Westendorf, Harry Ambler, Frank Delaney, and Washington Smith—all but Castello from Delavan. Performers from the village included George Madden, Mary Anne Madden, and George Sloman; and from Racine, Castello, of course; his stepson Harry and apprentice Johnny Castello; and his wife, Frances. Castello presented his trained horses and mules, and his family were all riders.

Coup had stored the 1870 chattels at properties he owned in Delavan. The wagons were at his home on Walworth Street; the horses and camels were pastured at his farm south of Delavan Lake. There were no menagerie animals on the 1870 circus, so the caged collection for the Barnum show was never in Wisconsin.

When it became time to move the property to Bridgeport, Connecticut, where the majority of the framing was accomplished, ten carloads of wagons, horses, and camels left Delavan on March 20. P. T. Barnum's circus became an eastern fixture thereafter and remained so until it moved to Florida in 1927.

Coup's management genius flowered once it had the backing of Barnum's name and money. His indefatigable energy was employed in every detail of the new show, and it needed to be, as supervising the operation of such a large operation had seldom been undertaken. The Barnum circus was the largest in the country, even in its first year of existence. Coup, whose previous experience on a large show had been as Older's assistant on the Yankee Robinson circus, was now faced with managing 175 men, 245 horses, 95 wagons, and 3 exhibition tents.

He first strove to increase efficiency—not to save money, but to move the circus each day to its advertised stand. The number of workmen he employed would overwhelm the hotel capacity of all but the largest cities the troupe visited. Coup had fold-down bunks constructed in the baggage wagons so that the men could sleep on the lot. There were twelve bunks in each wagon, thus sixteen wagons were so used. One wagon was fitted up to be a cookhouse or kitchen. A dining tent was also provided. The performers and staff stayed and ate in hotels, as was the convention.

The baggage stock were provided with tents, about eight of them, and were stabled on the lot, but the "hotel stock," that is, the performing horses, were still put up at hotel or livery stables. If the distance to the next day's stand was thirty or forty miles, the hotel stock were shipped by railroad.

Another operational change was to present three performances a day, in place of the time-honored matinee and evening showings. These were presented at 10 a.m., 2 p.m., and 8 p.m. and presumably had the potential to increase daily income by one-third. It was by such innovations that Coup proved his value to the partnership.

In 1872 the huge show was mounted on the railroads. Never before had a circus with a menagerie and all the supporting equipment and all the personnel and horses been transported in this fashion. In his autobiography, *Sawdust and Spangles*, Coup claimed credit for the idea. Barnum, in his autobiography, *Struggles and Triumphs*, said it was *his* idea. We will most likely never know who first suggested it, but we must point out that the only partner with experience in operating such a show was Dan Castello. Arthur Saxon, in his magnificent biography of Barnum, quite convincingly demonstrates that the old showman decided that rail transportation was the answer to the problem of moving between the larger cities, where the profit potential was greatest.

The purpose of the change was to increase the mobility of the company to the point that it could avoid the smaller towns that a wagon-borne circus had to visit if it was to perform every day. By making nightly moves of up to a hundred miles, the circus was able to perform where audiences were bound to be larger. This was conclusively demonstrated when the 1872 gross was over a million dollars, and again in 1873 when it was a million and a half.

Whatever the history of the idea, it was Coup's job to carry out the physical task of changing to the new system. First, he had to convince the railroads that it was possible to move a sixty-one-car train (in two sections) in daily traffic, stopping each day to unload and load again. He was amazed to discover that the flatcars used by the railroads were not of uniform size. Some were higher than others, some longer than others. This was true between railroads as well as within individual companies. The solution was to buy their own special-design show cars, and this was done in midseason of 1872.

As with the presentation of any new idea to an entrenched and operating industry, Coup faced the inability of railroad officials to understand his needs. What he wanted was to create a continuous platform of railcars upon which his wagons would enter at one end and be towed into place, one behind the other, until all were aboard. The unloading process would be an opposite movement. Each wagon was to be in the same place on the train after each loading. Stock cars for the horses and sleeping cars for the employees would be coupled in front of or behind the flatcars.

Just getting the brake wheels at the front of each flatcar removed so that there would be no impediment to the continuous movement of wagons onto and along the train first had to be accomplished by subterfuge. Once the train was loaded, the brake wheels were replaced, of course. One railroad official suggested that they load one car at a time, sidetrack it, and bring up another flatcar. Coup estimated that such a routine would require twenty-four hours to load the entire circus and rejected the idea.

And it was not just the railroad people who had to be indoctrinated. Coup's own workforce had to be trained in this new technique, for which there were no antecedents. In addition, he complained of being mentally fatigued by his partner's opposition to the scheme and his requests to abandon it. This is confusing to the researcher, for if Barnum suggested the adoption of railroad travel, why would he then turn against the idea as Coup sought to implement it? As yet, no commentator has satisfactorily answered this question.

After great effort—Coup said he literally did not change the clothes on his back for the first seven days—the process came together, and the railroad-borne circus was a matter of reality, and of success. Peter Sells of the rival Sells Bros. Circus said, "Taking rail ... came upon the circus fraternity like an avalanche." It is this event that secured Coup's fame as a manager and ensured him a place in the front ranks of circus men. It is the one thing that sticks in memory about his career; he put the Barnum show on rails.

Coup left the firm at the end of the 1875 season. For one thing, he was exhausted physically. He went to Europe for a rest. However, it is commonly reported that he was unhappy with Barnum's propensity to lend his name to circuses other than the one Coup had worked to glorify. In both 1872 and 1874 the elder partner had allowed other showmen to put the Barnum name on companies that were not successful. We have found no comment to this effect from either man and can only guess that it came from showmen's gossip. Both Barnum and Coup were always complimentary when speaking of one another, both during and after their association.

One source has said that Coup came away from the partnership with $250,000 in hand. If so, this was not the price he got from his share of the partnership, but his accumulated savings. He entered into several arrangements over the next few years. Among them was the New York Aquarium and the "Equescurriculum," a show of trained horses.

In 1879 Coup and some others financed W. C. Coup's United Monster Shows, a large circus that came to grief in 1882 because of a bad railroad accident on top of an unrewarding sojourn in the Southwest.

Coup's advertising in 1881 and 1882 made mention of his accomplishments, and though rife with hyperbole, as might be expected, it indicates what he personally felt were the high

Among the innovations of the 1871 Barnum show was the introduction of the name "courier" for the magazine-like advertisement that was distributed free by the thousands. The format had existed for a few years, but Barnum's advertising corps made it an indispensable part of the circus's advertising campaign. Courier, 1871, Circus World Museum.

points of his career to that time. Foremost of these was his abandoning the old "wagon shows" and putting the first railroad show on the road. This was factually incorrect but not too far from the truth. He claimed to have first planned and organized the great New York Hippodrome, omitting any reference to Barnum. This is understandable in view of the fact that he was competing with Barnum at the time, at least in the sense that they both had circuses on tour. He referred to his building the iron Equescurriculum in New York. He mentioned his building the New York Aquarium. All these undertakings bore Coup's stamp, and he was justly proud of his involvement in them. "Coup is the man to whom the public and profession are most indebted for all the radical improvements in the show profession in the last decade," said his 1881 press handouts.

In his autobiography Coup revealed many of his prejudices, and they shed some light on his character. Using the autobiography calls for some caution, as it was not a formal document in the usual sense. Apparently, at various times in his career, he wrote down some of his experiences with a view to publication, but at his death the notes were neither in order nor in a finished form. One Forrest Crissey organized the material, wrote a foreword, and published it as *Sawdust and Spangles* in 1901. The volume has odd pacing and some queer juxtapositions, and, of course, we don't know what Crissey discarded, yet it is one of the few collections of the reflective knowledge of a major nineteenth-century circus operator.

The violence connected with popular entertainment, especially in the South and West, was a matter of wonder to Coup. In his early days, while traveling with small circuses, he found the showmen to be a rough lot and the "sturdy sons of toil" to be the same. The locals came to the show lot eager to resent any imagined insult, and, failing to fight with the showmen, fought among themselves. "Not once a month, or even once a week, but almost daily, would these fights occur," he wrote.

Just as the Duke of Wellington called his soldiers "scum," Coup acknowledged that the circus workmen were mostly poor specimens of humanity. It was dirty, fatiguing work, by modern standards, yet it gave them a group standard of loyalty that was not available in farm labor or canal digging. Many of them followed the flag for years.

Coup was intrigued by the gullibility of the general public. He acknowledged that the rural population lived in practical isolation, "as if on a desert isle," he wrote. Their credulity was stretched to the limit by the claims and manipulations of the showmen, especially in the exhibits known as sideshows or "freak shows," as they came to be called. "The public loves to be humbugged," Barnum supposedly said, and every device was resorted to in satisfying this hunger. The populace, especially the country folk, were almost illiterate, and the mellifluous language of the posters and the profligacy of their distribution raised expectations to the highest level. Add to this the athletic demonstrations presented in the circus ring, the highly trained animals, and the comic antics of clowns, and there was an almost dizzying electricity on circus day. It is no wonder that in coming to the shows from the drudgery of everyday life, people often seemed to lose their heads.

THE MIGHTY MONARCH OF THE RAIL!

THE
W. C. COUP
NEW
UNITED MONSTER
SHOWS.

WAIT AND WATCH
FOR
THE BIG
ELEVEN 11 ELEVEN
DON'T MISTAKE
ITS DAY AND DATE

W. C. Coup's organizational skills and perfection of daily labor routines made the large railroad circus a reality. In a twist of fate, the failure of his most ambitious enterprise, his own New United Monster Shows, was precipitated by a railroad wreck incurred by the show in 1882. Courier, 1879, Circus World Museum.

"There are shows which made up to $50,000 a season through gambling schemes on circus lots," Coup once said. "I have been offered as high as $1,000 for the privilege to rob my patrons by camp followers … If I cannot run a show without a lot of gambling schemes attached to it, I'll stop running a show." And as far as has been discovered he kept to that vow.

In 1882 Coup's circus, W. C. Coup's New United Monster Shows, was framed in Augusta, Georgia. It was a large railroad-borne, three-ring show with a strong cast of performers. John F. Polacsek wrote a history of the circus in 1984 in which he pointed out that as a result of a wreck of the Coup train fifty miles north of Cairo, Illinois, the eventual demise of the show was ordained. Five employees had been killed, another thirty were injured, and the show temporarily lost the ability to earn revenue. Though the troupe went on to its destination in Detroit and even presented performances there, orders of attachment in favor of unpaid employees and suppliers caused its demise in August.

Coup, ever ready to expound his theories of show business, gave an interview to a *Detroit News* reporter while waiting in the city for the auction of his chattels. In it he claimed that other showmen imitated his ideas, such as using railroad trains for transport, using an advertising car, and instituting the two-ring format. Then he gave his opinion as to the proper way circuses should be presented. He would do away with expensive and exaggerated advertising and replace it with plain, honest announcements. He wanted to eschew the admittedly popular street parade, again because of the cost. He favored exhibiting in cities like Detroit for longer runs instead of the usual one-week stay. This, he maintained, would allow admission tickets to be much cheaper; he even advocated including streetcar fares in the price of the circus ticket. He was against having menageries, feeling that confining animals to closed cages was a cruel practice, and that long stands would allow exhibiting them in a more open and comfortable manner.

That these were revolutionary thoughts is obvious, and, as might be expected when espoused by a failed showman, they were ignored, but now they seem to be visionary; some of them were adopted over the next hundred years. Coup had come a long way from his roots in Wisconsin.

With the loss of his circus Coup was left with only his Delavan property and a great deal of debt. To his credit, he paid most of his creditors before he died. He sold his house in Delavan and based himself in New York after 1879. His wife had relatives in Beloit, Wisconsin, so they visited the area regularly, and the *Delavan Enterprise* often commented on his doings.

He remained active in show business, though not always as a proprietor. His name, like Dan Castello's, had luster, and he lent it to various shows of which he was a member, though not the owner. Coup died on March 4, 1895, and is buried in Delavan, which he once described as "the prettiest town on earth." He was so taken with Delavan that he once took Barnum there to look at it.

Louis E. Cooke, a turn-of-the-century showman, impressed by Coup's manners, dubbed him "the Chesterfield of the arenic world." The way in which he left the New York Aquarium is indicative of his convictions. He opposed his partner's idea of opening the building on Sunday. The argument reached obdurateness on both sides and was finally settled by the flipping of a coin. Coup lost, and he sold out his interest in a prosperous venture. He seems, in retrospect, to have lived an almost exemplary life. In researching his career, we found no one who spoke ill of him, certainly an anomaly in the rough-and-tumble business of popular entertainment.

BURR ROBBINS

In 1871, the same year that Messrs. Coup and Castello launched the P. T. Barnum circus, a man from Paw Paw, Michigan, bought a circus that was to become an important part of the Wisconsin entertainment pantheon.

Burr Robbins (1837–1908), a native of New York transplanted to Cleveland and then to Michigan, was the owner of a little sideshow with which he played county fairs. His ascension from a year of such work to the proprietorship of a circus followed a most unusual scenario. A man by the name of J. A. Wallace of Keokuk, Iowa, invested in a small show at Quincy, Illinois, on June 22, 1871. It was called John Stowe & Sons Great Western Circus. Wallace operated his new acquisition for just eleven days, one of the shortest circus careers in history. He was a deacon of his church in Keokuk, and once it was known that he was in show business, the church expelled him. In addition, his wife informed him that she would leave him if he persisted in the scheme. Faced with these ultimatums, combined with the poor business the circus was experiencing, Wallace drove it into Keokuk and laid it up on July 31. At this point Burr Robbins bought the property.

Robbins's life was compared by a writer in *Billboard* to that of Andrew Carnegie. Both men, he wrote, commenced life as poor boys, starting at the bottom rung of life's ladder and ascending to the top, accumulating millions. The comparison was apt but overdrawn. By the time Robbins acquired the little circus in 1871 he had been a waiter on a Great Lakes steamer, an actor with a stock company, a factory hand, a property man with the Spalding & Rogers circus, the leader of a failed concert company, a harvest hand in Illinois, the owner of a traveling panorama, a Civil War wagon master, the owner of two theatres in the oil country, and the operator of a boot and shoe store in Michigan. All this by the time he was thirty-two years old.

Robbins was born in Union, New York, on October 1, 1837. He left home at eighteen, partly because his parents wanted him to go to Western Reserve College and become a minister. In 1870 he bought the sideshow we spoke of, the outfit he was traveling with when he acquired the circus in mid-1871. Given the pressures that J. A. Wallace was under from church and wife, Robbins may have been able to consummate the sale quite inexpensively.

The title of the show was changed to Burr Robbins & Co.'s Circus and Museum, indicating the inclusion of the sideshow in the new company. John Stowe, who had lost the property in 1871, was the "& Co." of Robbins's effort. What little is known of the 1872 route out of Paw Paw includes Michigan, Indiana, and Ohio with a return to Paw Paw in the fall. During the winter Robbins enlarged the property twice over, evidence of a successful tour.

When the troupe left Paw Paw on April 28, 1873, for the summer, it consisted of sixteen baggage wagons, fifteen cages, six carriages for the performers, and

With hard-boiled business principles and practices, Burr Robbins built one of the larger railroad circuses of the nineteenth century. It was the largest in Wisconsin until the Ringling Bros. Circus went out for their third season on rails in 1892. Cabinet photograph, undated, courtesy Joanne Hathaway Sullivan.

three new tents. The big top, or main tent, was a 110-foot "round top" (i.e., 110 feet in diameter); the menagerie was housed in a 100-foot round top and the museum, or sideshow, in a 70-footer. (It had been but two years since separate tents were introduced for these three parts of the circus. P. T. Barnum and James E. Warner were the innovators in 1871.) One of the additions that Robbins had made was an advertising wagon with mirrored sides that traveled ahead of the show, carrying the bill posters. One hundred four horses and ninety workmen supplied the muscle.

There were sixteen performers, making Robbins's a midsize circus, an impressive improvement over his little sideshow of just two seasons earlier. Albert F. Aymar, rider and equestrian director, was the best-known name on the roster. The title in this season was Burr Robbins & Co.'s Moral Museum, Circus and Menagerie.

On June 8 the troupe crossed Lake Michigan from Grand Haven to Milwaukee to begin a long route in Wisconsin and Minnesota. They performed in Janesville, and something must have caught Robbins's eye in that town because at the end of the season, October 14, 1873, they put into Janesville, where they maintained their winter quarters for the next fourteen years.

The arrival of the show in Janesville was described by David Watt in 1913, and his words are summarized here:

> The circus was stored at the fairgrounds, where temporary buildings were
> built for the menagerie and horses and the men who were to be kept on for the
> winter. The two proprietors and their families found quarters at the Myers House
> and the Ogden House. They leased a stone building in the rear of City Hall,
> installed heating and temporary cages, and moved in the menagerie. The horses,
> 130 of them, were either pastured at the fairgrounds or put out to farmers to care
> for through the winter. The baggage wagons and cages were sent to the Hodge &
> Buchholz Carriage works for overhaul and repainting. A storeroom was rented,
> and four or five harness makers were set to work at repairing. All the groceries,
> feed, leather and lumber were purchased locally. The merchants of Janesville
> realized thousands of dollars because the town served as the winter quarters. In
> time, and up through the Great Depression of the 1930's cities vied for the privi-
> lege of hosting shows over the winter months.

John Stowe left the partnership during the winter of 1873. As sole owner, Robbins must have enjoyed his success, especially in looking back on such a varied career. He once said, when he was in the stock company playing walk-on parts in Cleveland, he had a sort of epiphany (not unusual to young men in such circumstances) in that he wanted to be a theatrical manager and devote himself to the business of public entertainment. His musical talents were apparently above the average. He was said to have had a strong and melodious voice and to have been proficient on the guitar, an instrument he played all his life. He was short-legged, round, and pleasant of face and had none of the usual theatrical vices, such as liquor, tobacco, or profligacy with money. This last stood him in good stead and allowed him to slowly build his business into a very successful one.

David Watt, ticket seller and treasurer of the circus beginning in 1878 and manager in 1880 and 1881, has left us the most detailed history of the Robbins show. He characterized the owner as a hard taskmaster, but one who taught him a basic knowledge that served Watt well in his later career. The first time that Watt was in charge of the show and assembled the wagon train for Robbins's inspection before leaving for the first performance of the season, Robbins spotted a problem on one wagon. Watt got an earful, which he reported as including the following: "I will have a man in your place next season if I have to pay him $1,000 a week."

Watt was being paid $10 a week, plus room and board, of course. He decided that he'd have to find new work in the next season but went on doing his job as he saw fit. However, it was not the last "curtain lecture" that he received. Robbins had other complaints. "Slower than molasses in January," he would say if the line at the ticket window got too long for his liking.

"He was not at all backward in telling me so," Watt recorded. "Occasionally, I would take an inning myself, and tell him a few things that you would be a long time hearing from a pulpit."

A few years later, after Watt had gone to the Adam Forepaugh circus, Robbins brought some friends to the Lake Front lot in Chicago to show them his "Old Steady," as he phrased it, and watch him sell tickets.

"It was with pride that Burr Robbins would tell his friends that he was the man that started me in the business," Watt wrote. "I learned early that there was only one way to deal with Burr Robbins, and that was to the last cent [for] he seemed to think it necessary to find fault about so often.

"One time ... he had been to Chicago for a few days, and came back to the show when I knew everything was going fine, and [he] found a good deal of fault. The breakfast had been too early, and no use in keeping the people with the show up most of the night. This pleased the performers to see Mr. Robbins taking their part, but all this made it hard for me ... I told him if I was to be held responsible for getting the show over the road, I would have to have the breakfast at the time I thought best. ...

"One time in particular, in the far west (i.e., Nebraska or Kansas), we had a thirty-two mile drive to make, and while the roads were supposed to be good, there were nine miles of this that was sandy, and would be a dead pull ... I ordered a 12 o'clock breakfast at the hotel, and when Mr. Robbins looked at the register he said, 'I want you to change your order for breakfast to two hours later.'

"I said, 'Mr. Robbins, I have been out with the livery man several miles on this road, and there is no part of it any too good, and the last nine miles is sand, and we will hit it after daylight, and when the sun commences to pour down, it will tell on the tired horses ...'

"After saying a few things that would not look well in print, he said, "Rather than have you talk the rest of the afternoon about it, go ahead and have your own way ...""

Watt wrote this thirty-five years after the events, but it is apparent that Robbins's treatment of him still rankled. However, Robbins had a managerial system that worked, as testified to by his success. Another aspect of his success was the absence of grifters and con men on the show. While this improved any show's reputation in the last quarter of the nineteenth century, a time when snake-oil sales and shortchanging were ubiquitous, it took time for such knowledge to sink into the public mind. "Vulgarity, personality, and politics ignored," Robbins advertised in 1873, addressing a common complaint about the content of clown routines.

One curious attitude, for a showman, was Robbins's avoidance of competition. Watt quoted him as saying that it was a big country, and there was plenty of room for everybody. Whether this dictated his going into the western states so often in the early years of the show isn't known. But even after he mounted the circus on the railroads, which freed him to cover more territory, he stayed with his modest Midwestern routes. He played Wisconsin every year, yet appeared but once in Milwaukee. He avoided Chicago and Detroit, though he played other venues in Illinois and Michigan numerous times. He never traveled east of Ohio or into the mid-South, common areas for Midwestern showmen to visit.

When John Stowe left the company in the winter of 1873, Robbins set about replacing the equipment that Stowe took as his share of the firm. The Great European Circus, a large eastern concern that had closed after the 1871 season, had offered a group of English-made parade wagons that Seth B. Howes had imported in 1864. These were magnificent vehicles, in the standard of the time, yet no one had offered for them when they were up for sale in 1872 and 1873. Robbins secured at least one of them for his 1874 show. This was a heavily carved and mirrored tableau wagon, which appeared in parade with a lion atop it, advertised as "a lion loose in the streets."

More important, he got his first elephant in 1874. She was advertised as Cleopatra but was better known as Babe and, according to one source, had come from the London Zoo. Incidentally, she was also the first elephant that the Ringling Brothers had, they having purchased it from the Sells Brothers in 1888.

The Miles Orton family was with Robbins in this season. Miles had all the privileges on the show (sideshow, concert, and candy sales). A cook tent was established, and the practice of stabling the baggage horses on the lot was begun. The performers, the staff, and the ring horses were still put up at hotels. There were 125 horses, 100 men, 18 cages, and 10 baggage wagons.

The last performance in 1874 was in Janesville on October 7. Ten days later the equipment was moved to a farm in Spring Brook, a mile south of town on the Rock River. Robbins had bought the 110-acre property from a Mrs. Doty. Over the summer he had a huge barn, a ring barn, a paint shop, and an animal house constructed. This was to be the winter quarters as long as Burr Robbins owned the circus. The Robbins household established itself in the former farmhouse.

Robbins's wife, Nettie, constantly traveled with the company and took tickets at the front door afternoons and evenings. It was she who counted up the house each evening, that is, matched the tickets with the receipts. Dave Watt opined that she spent more time on the lot than her husband, as he was called away on business from time to time. In 1880, the year that Robbins was home because of an injury he had suffered, she was the arbiter of any questions that arose, though Watt was the manager. The Robbinses had two children, a son named Burnett and a daughter named China.

The 1875 season saw the introduction of a new bandwagon from the shop of Hodge & Buchholz of Janesville. It served Robbins until it was sold to the Ringlings in 1889. Miles Orton and his family were again on the program, and once more Orton himself had the privileges. There were forty more horses, thirty more workmen, and seven more cages than in 1874.

Even with these increases, Robbins's circus remained but midsize, dwarfed by the large shows that came out of the East. He had 25 cages in 1875; Howes's Great London had 32, DeHaven had 36, and Forepaugh had 48. It was the beginning of "the Golden Age of the Circus," as we mentioned (more properly, it was the age of commercial growth in the whole American economy), and in the labor-intensive businesses such as traveling shows with their cohorts of cheap labor, expansion was limited only by the ability to manage it. The majority of the larger companies were copying W. C. Coup's 1872 adoption of railroad transportation in order to avoid playing the small towns. But these big shows limited their excursions. A line drawn from St. Louis to Chicago would measure the westward limit of most routes. Robbins,

The staff of the Burr Robbins cookhouse is posed in front of their tent. The cook, who is seated, is flanked by mostly youthful assistants who prepared food for cooking and then delivered it to the tables in the dining tent. Card photograph, circa 1887, Algona, Iowa, Circus World Museum.

almost from the beginning of his circus career, moved westward, playing in Wisconsin, Minnesota, Iowa, and Kansas. In one season, 1879, they spent almost the entire year in small-town Illinois.

Burt Webster of Delavan traveled with Burr Robbins's circus in 1875, and this was his take on the life:

> You had to have a strong constitution to go out with a wagon show. It was often easier walking than riding in the wagons over rough roads. Sundays were usually spent on a longer ride as we never showed on Sunday, and the long jumps were left for that day. Sometimes, early in the season, we had to get out of the wagons and walk to keep from freezing.

Webster lasted just one season with the circus, but he was not typical of the workmen. Watt once wrote:

> … even back in the days of the wagon show, when it was work all day and travel all night, many people followed the business year after year. They went through hardships that they would not think of going through in any other line of work, usually in the spring and late fall, when cold rains and deep mud made it almost impossible to get from town to town, and arrive in time to give two performances. You would think that after one experience of this kind it would be the last season many of the men would continue in this line of work, and yet the next spring, long before starting out, ninety per-cent of them would always be on hand.

For 1876 Robbins's title was Robbins Great American and Rentz' German Allied Shows. Rentz's identity, if he existed, isn't known. There was a famous Circus Renz in Germany, and Robbins's routes led through country heavily settled by German immigrants, so he may have been betting on the possible recognition of the Rentz name. That title lasted one year and was then changed to Burr Robbins' American and German Allied Shows, which sufficed until 1882. Admission was fifty cents, twenty-five for children; soft cushioned seats with backs and footrests were offered for twenty-five cents extra. The roster included some well-known names, such as the Lee family (six of them) and George Bushnell, recently on Barnum. King Sarbro, a Japanese wirewalker, contributed his troupe of jugglers and acrobats. Madame Leon entered the lion's cage each day, and a man named Dodworth did the same for the hyenas. A small elephant, Mogul, was added to the menagerie.

One source has reported that in 1876 the circus traveled 3,133 miles and visited 137 towns. The average move from place to place was $22^1/2$ miles. Some of the daily expenses were for three tons of hay ($10 per ton), 120 bushels of oats (35 cents per bushel), and license fees that averaged $75. These three items, over the season, cost $21,621.

As for management, a circus the size of Robbins's was in the same position as a minor league baseball team is today. As soon as a man gained experience and proved his ability, he was swept up by a larger organization that could offer a higher salary. Without a thorough investigation, it appears that Robbins had this problem, as the turnover in staff positions was continuous. On the other hand, he was a hard taskmaster, as we've mentioned. Conversely, some key heads of departments were with him over several seasons. The general agent (George K. Steele), the treasurer (David Watt), the boss hostler (Spencer Alexander), and the band-master (John Smith) were all able to live with Robbins's style.

The Montgomery Queen Circus was auctioned in Louisville in February 1878. Robbins was there and bought several animals. He was interviewed by a newspaper reporter, who asked him if the Queen auction signified dull times in the circus business. Robbins's answer was a definite no; it was poor management that caused the failure.

In that same winter he purchased ten Arabian camels, which were featured in the grand entree titled "The Uprising of the Arabs." Richard Brooks appeared in the ring with the two elephants, and King Sarbro, the Japanese acrobat, did a slide for life backward on a wire stretched from the center pole to the ring bank. Hiram Marks's family of riders (Minnie, Sally, and Willie) were on the show, as was Pete Conklin, the famous clown, then in his twenty-second year before the public. They had 20 ring horses, 150 baggage horses, 35 drivers, and 20 canvasmen and were easily the largest circus in the West.

David Watt, who had been running a livery stable in Janesville, began his four-year career as Robbins's ticket seller and treasurer in 1878 (though Nettie Robbins still counted up the house). In 1912 he started a weekly series of articles on his circus career in the *Janesville Gazette* that ran for nine years, supplying much information on the Robbins Circus and on Robbins himself.

In 1878 they went from Wisconsin into Iowa, Nebraska, and Kansas. Towns were few and far between in the western states. They often went from county seat to county seat in one night because there were no towns in between. One night they drove fifty-five miles. In such cases they were off the lot by 9:00 p.m. and drove all night. Breakfast was what we now call a brown-bag affair. People drove to the show from as far away as sixty miles and stayed for both performances. There was no newspaper advertising, no billboards, and no lot and license expense in these reaches. The net profit for the season was $90,000. Watt said the show itself was worth $45,000, thus the return on investment was 100%.

The circus traveled on sixty-two wagons in 1879, among them a new organ wagon built by Hodge & Buchholz. It was in this season that the company spent four months visiting the small towns in Illinois. Of southern Illinois Watt said, "The towns, and even the country, presented a desolate appearance, and yet everyone seemed to have money to visit the circus." What he was observing was the almost universal need to be entertained that the nineteenth-century populace shared with the people of today. With few holidays, and only Sunday as a break from the unremitting toil of farming, the general public seized the opportunity to visit the circus. "This proved to be one of the biggest seasons that the Burr Robbins show ever had," Watt observed.

In January 1880, Robbins suffered a near-fatal accident. He was returning to the farm from Janesville on his private steam-yacht when it hit a bridge, trapping his head between the yacht's boiler and the bridge. It nearly separated his scalp from his head. For weeks he was expected to die. Friends covered the street in front of his house with wood shavings to deaden the noise of passing wagons. Nettie Robbins, with Watt's assistance, took over preparations for the 1880 season. Opening day was May 1 in Janesville, and Burr Robbins attended the performance. When he walked slowly into the tent, the crowds erupted in cheer after cheer.

As in all the preceding seasons, 1880 was spent visiting the small towns. Robbins himself did not join the company until midseason. They played in Delavan on May 3. That night it began to rain, and it continued for twenty-two days. However, coming as it did at planting time, the rain abetted the receipts, as the farmers, unable to work their fields, went to the show. The roads were a muddy mess. On one move from town to town the troupe paid out nearly $100 to farmers to hire their teams to help get the wagons over the road. Many of the horses had colds, especially the lighter ring stock. The loss of horses by an overland circus, moving every day in all kinds of weather as they did, seem prodigious to a modern reader. Sandy roads, hilly country, and indifferent feed all contributed to fatigue and illness. If an animal foundered, it was taken out of the team and left by the roadside. The performer's carriages or carryalls, which left later than the baggage train, would sometimes come to town with two or three of these tired animals tied behind. In 1878, according to Watt, on one stretch of very bad road leading into Anamosa, Iowa, seven of the baggage horses died from exhaustion. As a consequence of this attrition, overland circuses bought horses as they moved.

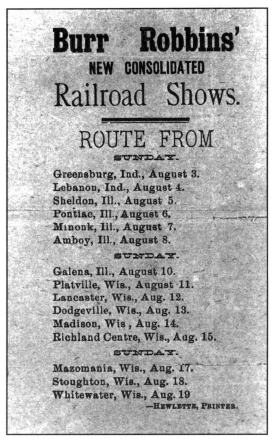

Circus owners like Burr Robbins printed and distributed "route cards" as a means of informing the troupe, and their families at home, of the impending engagements of the circus. Known to have been issued by 1875, they are still being sent out by shows today. Route card, 1885, courtesy Joanne Hathaway Sullivan.

The wear and tear on man and beast and equipment that characterized the wagon show could be alleviated by railroad travel. The transportation of circuses in America was carried out successively by wagon, steamboat, railroad, and motor truck. Each of these methods required different operating procedures, but all were alike in purpose, enabling the circuses to reach the places where they could present their wares to the public.

In the 1850s it became possible, because of the increase in trackage, for a circus to travel by rail for an entire season. Several entrepreneurs took advantage of this improvement. The routes of the railroads and those of the circus were established to connect centers of population, a serendipitous situation for the showmen.

The earliest rail movements were those in which the performers were moved short distances while the horses and wagons went overland. The next step was to put the entire circus on a train. Because of the expense, such circuses were originally limited in size. They carried no wagons and thus had no menageries or parades, just as was true of the steamboat shows. They hired local drayman to transport their properties from the train to the circus lot, and they carried their ring stock in boxcars. The restrictions in size made railroad-borne troupes poor relatives of the big wagon shows, such as Burr Robbins's. With 50 or so wagons, 150 to 200 horses, plus a dozen cages of animals, the wagon show dwarfed the railers. The discrepancies in size led Robbins to advertise, "This stupendous organization is not a railroad establishment, but travels by wagon; 268 horses are used to transport it through the country, also, quite an army of men is employed, about 250 in number." Most of the wagon shows used this or similar language to distinguish themselves from their smaller brethren.

In 1881 Burr Robbins chose to make the change; fortunately, he had the money to do it. What he lacked was experience in managing a railroad show, a quantity much different from that of leading an overland company. He entered into a partnership with Erasmus D. Colvin, a man whom Charles Day once characterized as knowing everyone in the circus business, as well as being frugal and a shrewd investor. This sounds like Robbins himself; they should have made an ideal combination, but they did not. Colvin had been manager of several large overland shows, George F. Bailey's and Adam Forepaugh's among them. He had also run two railroad circuses, those of Montgomery Queen and W. C. Coup. Colvin assumed the position of manager, and the partners purchased a twenty-one-car train from the Chicago Union Rolling Stock Co.

For unknown reasons, Robbins and Colvin did not see eye to eye when it came to operating the new concern. It may have been that Robbins could not make the adjustment from overland to rail travel. In any case, Watt, who had been replaced by Colvin, was called back to the company, and both partners left the concern for the balance of the season. It is at this point that we first see Robbins's desire to divest himself of the circus.

Over the winter of 1881–1882, having bought Colvin's interest, Robbins sold the show to O. P. Myers and John S. Shorb for $65,000, receiving a down payment of $10,000. When the new owners failed to keep up payments to their lithograph supplier, they were forced into foreclosure in July 1882. The property was auctioned in Louisville in September, and Robbins bought it. He had to pay $25,000 essentially to reclaim his own chattels.

Mounted on twenty-one 50-foot cars with 120 wagons (including 18 cages), 2 elephants, and a hippopotamus, Burr Robbins's New Consolidated Railroad Shows went out of Janesville in 1883 as a corporation. The owner of the *Janesville Gazette*, R. L. Colvin (no relation to Erasmus), sold his newspaper and became treasurer. George K. Steele, general agent since 1875, also invested. Robbins, in a newspaper interview, said the show was the third largest in the country, putting only the Barnum and Forepaugh companies ahead of his. The one important change on the 1883 version of the firm was the adoption of the two-ring format, a measure, as we stated earlier, of crowd control.

Robbins celebrated his fourteenth season in the business in 1884, and it was the first one in which he lost money. The year itself saw what economists define as "Grant's Last Panic," a time of much concern about the relative value of specie and paper money. It was a period fraught with speculation and a great deal of stock manipulation. To businesses the Panic was a trifle, as prices were already so low they couldn't go lower, but the fear engendered by all the bankruptcies and bank failures made the public cautious. Popular entertainment can thrive only when discretionary funds are widely available; circus tickets are never high on the list of necessities.

The next season, 1885, was another bad one for showmen, but Robbins made a profit despite an enlarged daily expense of $1,500. J. J. Nathans, an old circus proprietor and a Barnum partner, when asked once what to do when business was slow, answered, "Lower admissions." Robbins did this, going from fifty to twenty-five cents. It unsettled the competition but apparently delighted the public. He advertised, "More and better features than ever before in the tented field. A miniature world gathered beneath the canvas skies, and all for 25 cents, half the usual price."

In 1887 railroad rates on major lines were increased, and when Robbins went to Milwaukee to "make rates" with the operating companies, he discovered that the new rates would make a difference to him of $400 to $600 more per haul. He was quoted in the *New York Clipper* as saying that the business would be killed in two years. This was another clue to his desire to retire. As it came to pass, such increases were much more modest than threatened, because of the contractual arrangements. The railroads wanted to penalize the short-haul customers, not the steady contracts the circus represented.

The Burr Robbins street parade is forming on an unidentified show grounds. A line of elegantly painted cages is on the left and the hippo den is on the far right. The lead bandchariot, with Harry Armstrong's band, is in the middle. Other wagons, chariots, riders, and horses were included in the daily march. Card photograph, 1887, Dixie Hicks Gift, Circus World Museum.

One of Robbins's big attractions in 1887 was a stuffed right whale, which in life, the advertisements read, weighed fifty tons. One observer said it was carried in a fifty-foot railroad car; another said it was made of papier-mâché. The advertising read, "This overwhelming mammalian wonder is exhibited with magnificence in the greatest private railroad car ever used, equaling two ordinary cars in length."

The performances, according to one writer, "… are chaste and pure in character, and heretofore unexcelled." During his reign as owner of Wisconsin's largest circus Robbins conducted his show on a clean and honest basis. No games of chance, nor other kinds of grift, such as shortchanging, were allowed on the grounds, and few reports of trouble with local "toughs" are found in the records. With the exception of one or two small Delavan circuses, the records of Wisconsin circuses are remarkably free of obnoxious practices.

By 1887 Robbins was fifty years old and a very wealthy man apparently weary of circus life. He owned real estate all across the country, forty parcels in Chicago alone. In the winter of 1887–1888 he made an agreement with one Thomas Grenier to trade the circus for Grenier's Garden, a Chicago theatre.

Though he invested in a circus in 1889, he had no part in its management, and he spent the rest of his life looking after his money. His mark on his chosen career was firm; he had built one of the half-dozen largest circuses in the country. Until the Ringling brothers of Baraboo emerged as successful entrepreneurs in the 1890s, Burr Robbins had the distinction

A clown cart led the second bandwagon in the middle of the Burr Robbins parade. A ring horse, racing chariots, an elephant, and other vehicles trail behind them down the main thoroughfare of Algona. Card photograph, circa 1887, Algona, Iowa, Dixie Hicks Gift, Circus World Museum.

of being Wisconsin's leading impresario. After his death in 1908 a writer said that like John Robinson and Adam Forepaugh, Robbins had accumulated a fortune by judicious spending, concentration on business, and honest dealings. He left an estate of over $2 million, which in 1990 would have amounted to $22 million. This was an awesome accumulation for a man who started out in 1870 with a magic lantern and a caged wildcat.

THE HALL FAMILY

The saga of George Washington "Popcorn George" Hall (1837–1918), taking place as it did in a settled country with a mature money system and roads and newspapers to cohere its population, has none of the appeal of a pioneer exploit. Hard work, not survival, was his motif. He claimed that he had a lot of fun and that he had participated in a fascinating game, the art of the showman. That he made his living in a field that was considered less than acceptable socially, filled with acts of dubious morality and condemned by pulpit and press alike, bothered him not a whit. In the Evansville of his day—he lived there from 1880 until his death in 1918—he was considered a leading citizen, always responding to community needs and supportive of local endeavors. News of his adventures in Mexico and the Caribbean and his struggles in the "wild west" of that time was transmitted by his local agent to the townspeople and duly reported in the newspapers. How much envy his life stirred in the shopkeepers and farmers of Rock County we cannot say, of course, but none, we are sure, were ignorant of this bustling showman in their midst. And it didn't stop with him, for his children and grandchildren were showmen as well, and because of them Evansville rivaled Delavan of the preceding generation as a circus center.

When he was seventy-six years old, in 1913, Hall said to a reporter, "My schooling was sadly neglected. I was so crazy to run off with a show that I never had half a common school education. The last time I went to school was one winter when I was sixteen years old." What he didn't say was that when he was sixteen he'd already had six years of circus experience. Had he been the scion of a circus family, brought up in the business from babyhood, this would not be unusual. But Hall's father was a New England machinist, and he and his wife maintained a proper working-class family household. When George first left at the age of ten to be a peanut seller on Nathan Howes's New York Circus in 1848, he didn't stay away but returned home to spend the winter, as would any dutiful son.

He had as peripatetic a circus career as there ever was. For over fifty years he partook of almost every aspect of the genre. He was a seat seller, a privilege man, a museum operator, an animal trainer, and a circus owner. He invented the popcorn ball and the popcorn brick. He introduced the ten-cent circus. And he founded a family dynasty that operated entertainments of various types for a hundred years.

First in Wisconsin—at Magnolia—in 1860, he based his operations in Evansville after 1880. He subsequently had shows on the road almost every year until a final effort in 1910. Some of them were upright concerns, some

The flair of a circus impresario, along with his own personality, comes through in this portrait of "Popcorn George" Hall. It may date from before 1880, when he was awarded a medal by the Memphis fire chief for giving the generous proceeds from a benefit performance to the women and children of the city after a fire there. Tintype, undated, Mrs. Frank E. Hall Gift, Circus World Museum.

had grift, and almost all of them made money. He made it a habit to invest each season's profits in real estate and claimed that he never sold any of it. To that reporter to whom he outlined his lack of schooling, he recounted that he owned five farms in Wisconsin, fourteen rental houses in Evansville, $20,000 worth of property in Tampa, Florida, and a half-block of business property in Denver.

He claimed that he was not good at figures, and his daughter Jessie said he didn't have much of an accounting system. When he was on tour, he would send money by freight line to his bank in Evansville in tin cans, cigar boxes, gunny sacks, or whatever container was at hand. She told of leaving one of his suits behind once, and her father making her go back a hundred miles by freight train caboose to retrieve it. When she gave it to George, he started pulling many hundred-dollar bills from it.

He was called "Popcorn George" through much of his career, at first as a nickname but later to distinguish him from other showmen bearing that most common name. (At one time there were five circuses on tour bearing the Hall name.) He garnered this appellation through his career as a popcorn seller in the off-season, peddling on the streets of New York and on the trains out of Concord, New Hampshire. Popcorn, while known in the West, was a new delicacy to easterners (seemingly, only western farmers grew it), and their appreciation of it helped line the boy's pocket. He supplied hotels in New York City with popcorn, which the dining rooms served as dessert. During this period, the 1850s, he claimed, he invented both the popcorn ball and the popcorn brick. At one time he apparently had fifteen employees.

Hall was born in Lowell, Massachusetts, on December 5, 1837. He married Sarah Wilder in Concord in 1855, at age eighteen. Four children were born of this union, three of whom were subsequently in the circus. His father moved to a farm in Magnolia, Wisconsin, near Evansville, in 1859, and George followed him there. By that time he had attached himself to several circuses. If we read his list of them correctly, they would include Franconi's Hippodrome, Jim Myers, Sloat & Shepard, Joe Pentland, and Dan Rice. The problem with sorting out his affiliations arises from the fact that he didn't work for the circuses he traveled with. He was a privilege man, either a candy stand or sideshow operator, and thus was not usually listed as a member of any of the companies.

Living in New York in the winters, Hall applied himself to the popcorn business. In summers he went out with whatever show would have him. He came west with the 1860 R. Sands' Circus, owned by James Foshay, and later moved his family from New York to Wisconsin. Foshay's circus wintered in Chicago and set out from there in 1861, and George Hall was with it. In 1862 he was with the Mabie show out of Delavan; in 1863 it was George F. Bailey & Co., an eastern concern then on a Midwestern tour.

The year 1864 marked his first season as a circus proprietor. He spent almost $10,000 to frame a circus and menagerie, and lost almost all of it because he traveled in one of the wettest years "ever turned on," as he put it; "Didn't do enough business to pay for feed." However, by closing down and taking his sideshow out of Wisconsin to join another circus, he was able to close the season with a $5,000 profit. (He said it was Jim French's Circus he joined, but there was no French circus in 1864.) He "hibernated" in Madison that winter.

As often happens with people recalling their past, Hall confuses us with his dating of events. He planned to join Dan Castello, he claimed, in the year that Castello came out of St. Paul on a steamboat. As we've shown, that was 1864. But he said he joined Orton instead and headed for Omaha. That was also 1864. Yet his recital of his failure in Wisconsin he dates after 1863, his year with George Bailey. In trying to reconstruct this seeming conundrum, we can offer that after his failure in western Wisconsin he went with Orton's Circus, not French's. In the trans-Mississippi West of that year the bushes were infested with guerrillas, and one of Hall's comments was that they kept their knives sharpened so they could cut harness and run in case their horses were in danger of being stolen.

He attached his sideshow to Frank Howes's Champion Circus for 1865. We use the term "sideshow" generically, as Hall's offering was an exhibition of animals, not of the human curiosities that one usually associates with the term. He had a great affinity for animals and trained many over the course of his career. Most of the circuses he allied himself with had no menageries, so his presence on the lot was accepted, but not in those cases where his presence was seen as competing with their own sideshows. These would attempt to drive him

In addition to a complete circus, George Hall, Sr., also fielded sideshows and wild animal presentations on other show lots and at agricultural fairs. Here's the impressive bannerline of the Hall animal show. Photograph, undated, courtesy Eager Free Public Library, Evansville, Wisconsin.

away, threatening him (once with pistols), but he was not one to back down. If he couldn't set up on the circus lot, he located near it.

He began the 1866 season with "Old Man Orton," as he phrased it. This was Hiram Orton, who helped his sons operate what had been his circus. It is obvious from the record that Hall didn't hesitate to leave a show if business wasn't up to standard. In this season he switched from Orton to Dan Castello's Great Show and had a very successful year. In 1867 he was again with Castello (the title was Barnum, Van Amburgh & Castello), for whom he presented a lion act.

The next two years, according to his narrative, were spent with the Great Eastern Circus. We fail to find such a concern in 1868 or 1869. The Great Eastern was on tour in 1872 and 1873, and it must be that Hall confused his affiliations. One source says he spent some years with J. A. Johnson and John McKinstrie, Kansas showmen of poor reputation. Their circus was called the Great Western. It may be this that Hall referred to.

Most daunting of all to the researcher is the fact that George W. Hall does not appear, as employee or privilege man, with any known show during most of the decade of the 1870s. He attached his Great California Exposition to fellow Evansville citizen Bradley Chapin's circus in 1874 and is found in St. Louis on his way to Texas in 1878. His first marriage ended in divorce, and in 1875 he married Mary Louise Tolen in St. Louis. That fact was published in the *New York Clipper*, and it is one of the few references to him we've found until 1880, when he established headquarters in Evansville and spent the winter showing his "talking pig" in Chicago. This animal was one of a series of pigs the Halls, father and son, presented over the years, but what constituted the talking is nowhere in the records. In 1882 Popcorn was on tour in upper Michigan and that fall opened Col. Geo. W. Hall's American Museum on Water Street in Milwaukee. This was a sideshow operation featuring unusual people and animals. In 1883, he framed a show called Hall's Great Western, which was mounted in a railroad car purchased from Burr Robbins.

George Sr.'s 1884 circus opened in Milwaukee and became a one-car railroad show traveling along the Mississippi River. It reached Jacksonville, Florida, in late December and boarded ship for the West Indies in January 1885. Upon their return to the United States in the summer, the company was sold to Silas Dutton and George W. DeHaven, but Hall kept the sideshow privilege. Though it was titled G. W. Hall's Circus and Menagerie, the company continued under DeHaven's ownership and management.

The 1886 season proved to provide a great deal of excitement, beginning with the circus's presence in Galveston during the great fire there that year. Hall said they had to move the show five times to avoid the flames. In Mexico, which they crossed from the Gulf to El Paso, they found themselves in the midst of an insurrection in Monterrey, as a result of which they were besieged for eight days, unable to move. It was their intent to get to San Francisco before the Sells brothers arrived there, but another misfortune, an outbreak of smallpox, caused them to head north. Banking facilities were almost nonexistent in Mexico at that time, so the company had to carry its money with it. DeHaven appealed to the Mexican government, and a detachment of soldiers was provided to travel with the circus for protection. They finally closed the show and shipped back to Evansville.

A man by the name of C. H. Bingley went out of business in late 1886. Hall seems to have combined the animals from the defunct firm (Bingley & Stevens Bros.) and added them and Bingley's name to his title for 1888 and 1889, thus going on tour as G. W. Hall's Circus and Bingley's English Menagerie in those two seasons. However, when the company went broke in Atlanta, Georgia, in March of 1889, it was disclosed that "Popcorn George" owned none of it. H. C. Stevens of Chicago was the person who settled the claims in 1890; he and his brother, A. P. Stevens, had been Bingley's partners. An interesting sidelight to this failure is that the animals were purchased by an Atlanta citizen and provided the original stock of the Atlanta Zoo.

In the fall of 1889 Popcorn formed a partnership with Sam McFlinn to operate a sixteen-car railroad outfit, McFlinn & Hall's New York Circus. McFlinn (1852?–1911), clown turned proprietor just two years prior to this, owned Sam McFlinn's European Circus in 1888.The partnership lasted until January 1892 but was revived in 1896. We know little about most of these shows, because they toured so far from the large eastern cities where show business news was reported.

This is the performance cast of a George W. Hall, Sr., circus, including clowns, acrobats,
and a rider. The professions of some can be determined by their wardrobe, such as the clowns
(makeup), the rider (with riding crop), and the acrobats (waist sashes).
Card photograph, undated, Circus World Museum.

Hall's 1892 effort, G. W. Hall & Son's New United Railroad Shows, was briefly noted by Orin C. King in his massive compendium of the circus in Kansas. The title suggests that George Jr. and Charles Hall were members of the company. Daughter Jessie Hall was the snake charmer. The most telling item in King's account is a newspaper comment that a redeeming feature of Hall's Circus was that "The usual army of gamblers was not along."

Both of Popcorn's sons had their own circuses by 1893, so his "Railroad Shows" reverted to a one-man operation. He reverted even further in 1894 by framing one of his animal sideshows and playing at county fairs. The rise of agricultural fairs in western states was, of course, a product of increased settlement as well as a recognition of the importance of stock breeding and crop improvement. It soon became possible for someone like Hall to follow a regular circuit of such events. In some seasons he went out with a circus until fall, then took a sideshow to fairs.

In 1894, after forty-seven years in the business, "Popcorn George" bought another circus. It belonged to a man named E. F. Davis and had opened in New Orleans in February of that year, experienced a poor season in Texas, and was delivered to Hall in Cincinnati in the fall. Davis had a leased elephant called Empress. On the day she arrived on Hall's lot she attacked Hall as he was feeding his own two elephants. She knocked him unconscious, and in

Local residents turned out on "Circus Day" to observe the arrival and unloading of "Popcorn George" Hall's four- or five-car railroad circus. The circus equipment was "gillied" from the train to the show grounds on local rented drays or knockdown wagons owned by the show. Photograph, circa 1893, Las Vegas, New Mexico, courtesy Museum of New Mexico, Santa Fe, New Mexico, negative #9494.

attempting to crush him pressed him into the ground, breaking his hip. He walked with a crutch thereafter. In typical fashion, Hall offered the lessor, the Empire Printing Company of Chicago, $1,000 for the beast from his hospital bed. This was a quarter of what elephants brought at the time. To avoid being sued, the company let him have her.

Hall retired, for the first time, after the 1894 season, but found himself back at it in February 1896 when his son Charles, who was on the road with Sam McFlinn, died suddenly in Meridian, Mississippi. Charles was only thirty years old and was carried away by pneumonia. The father went south to join McFlinn in the operation. Frank Macart, Hall's son-in-law, and daughter Jessie were with the show and had been since its inception in 1891. Hall's second wife, Mary Louise, and their daughter, Mabel, were there as well. The company visited Mexico and California.

In 1897 Col. George W. Hall's New United States Railroad Shows, on eight cars, passed through Kansas in August, thus coming under the eye of Orin King, circus historian, who has read all the nineteenth-century Kansas newspapers. It seems that the show in the arena was a good one, but that the activities of the grifters on the outside of the tent were shameful. More newspaper space was given to these crooked schemes than to the performance. Hall went on south to join McFlinn, and they entered Mexico on November 1. They returned to Evansville and closed the circus in May 1898. Hall then retired for the second time, selling his railroad cars to a carnival company.

Unable to stand idleness, Hall took out a wagon show in 1900, and his 1901 and 1902 shows were both on rails, on five cars in the former year and ten in the latter. The 1902 edition had two rings, his first such arrangement. After this season he retired again, in the sense that he promised to do so several times (in 1894 and 1899), but as he once said, "Every spring it just seemed as if I must get on the road." In 1909 he framed a large wagon show, and in 1910 he organized a four-car show, Tiger Bill's Wild West and Col. Hall's Consolidated Shows, which began the season by playing what were called "the Chicago lots." These were various places near Chicago that small circuses had visited for some time, avoiding downtown locations, possibly to circumvent the need to "take care of" city officials. These locations were still popular in the 1940s.

Hall retired to the winter quarters, where he still had many animals, and tended to his farming operation and his real estate. He would lease animals to other showmen, train cat acts, and generally keep abreast of show business until he died in 1918. His obituary in the *Evansville Review* said, "Mr. Hall was what is known as a fighter, and whether it was in fighting financial vicissitudes, an angered mob, or an infuriated beast, his self possession and strong personality always carried him to a successful and victorious conclusion." As had Matthew

Following in his father's footsteps, George W. Hall, Jr., started his career at the tender age of eight and had his own sideshow operation when he was twenty-six. By the time he reached thirty-five he had made his first attempt at circus operation with his brother-in-law. Cabinet photograph, undated, courtesy Eager Free Public Library, Evansville, Wisconsin.

Buckley of Delavan, George Hall delivered to his progeny a legacy in field show operation that they carried on for three generations after his demise.

The eldest of these was George Jr. (1857–1930), whose first circus experience, outside of living at the winter quarters, was in 1865, when he accompanied his father on the Frank Howes Champion Circus. He presumably kept at this, learning the trade, until 1873, when he went out on his own, selling popcorn at the Union Stock Yards in Chicago. He went with Buckley's Hippodrome in 1874, and the next year he started selling popcorn balls at county fairs.

George Jr.'s first sideshow was placed on a Joe Parson circus, from Darlington, Wisconsin, probably in 1883. By this time George Sr. had taught his son the popcorn business, sideshow oration, and sideshow operation, all of it being knowledge from a master. In 1884 and 1885, the son had a sideshow on the fledgling Ringling Brothers Circus. He then took his show to Priest's Pavilion Show (1886), Bartine's Circus (1888), Eph Ferguson (1889), and Whiting Brothers (1890). All this moving from show to show was mandated by the short lives of the circuses, excepting Bartine, and, of course, the Ringling brothers.

George Jr.'s sister, Jessie (1871–1959), had married Frank Macart, a talented wirewalker and clown, and the two men were the owners of George Jr.'s first circus in 1892. It was titled Hall & Macart's Circus. The introduction of Macart into our narrative brings together one of the great European circus families, the Ginnetts, and the Evansville Halls. Frank was the son of Marie Macarte (1826–1892), one of the most famous of nineteenth-century equestriennes. Born Marie Ginnett in Paris, she married a performer named McCarty or McCarthy, and twisted the name to a French spelling (apparently pronounced McCarty). She made her American debut in 1845 under Rufus Welch and returned to England in 1848 upon news of an inheritance. According to the *New York Clipper* she was done out of the expected wealth and returned to riding in 1863. She was still in the ring in the 1880s.

George W. Hall Jr.'s Trained Animal Show went on tour in 1893 and was essentially his concern until 1905. At that time, or near to it, his wife, Lida, who had shared his career, became ill, and George decided that it would be easier on her if he switched to presenting animal shows on carnivals. By easier, we assume that he meant that the one-week-or-longer stands made by carnivals were not as arduous as the daily traveling of a wagon-borne circus. He did this until 1912, then retired, Lida being too ill to travel by this time (she died in 1917). After her death George settled into a pattern of working only fairs.

He said in an interview in 1922, "I have been in show business fifty-nine years. I never came home for want of money, and borrowed only $50 to get out one spring." He died in Whitewater, Wisconsin, at seventy-four in 1930.

Charles S. Hall did not make an enduring mark in the circus business except to have one of the few known Hall family show failures. He died prematurely, causing his father to take over the property. Photograph, undated, courtesy Eager Free Public Library, Evansville, Wisconsin.

George Jr.'s brother Charles (1864–1896) was also introduced to sideshow management by their father, at some time in the 1870s. The first position we find for him away from George Sr. is as sideshow manager on the 1889 King & Franklin Circus out of Indiana. Charles Hall's New Railroad Shows, a three-car affair, was organized by George Sr. in 1891 and included in its cast Jessie Hall Macart and her husband, Frank. Jessie had become a snake charmer, as they are still called, exhibiting reptiles in the sideshow. Her son, Walter Gollmar Jr., describes her as being extremely knowledgeable about them and acquiring a reputation as a "snake doctor." She would take in sick specimens and nurse them back to health. Sideshow and circus people would send her their ailing snakes for treatment, even after she had retired from exhibiting.

Charles Hall had one of the few failures documented in the Hall family; this was in 1894. Business was so bad, because of the Panic of 1893, that he had to fold his circus without paying salaries. He joined a man named Showers and changed the title to Hall & Showers for 1895. In the fall of that year, Hall combined with Sam McFlinn, his father's former partner, for a southern tour under the title McFlinn & Hall's Railroad Shows. In February 1896 Charles contracted pneumonia. He died, as we said, in Meridian, Mississippi, and Hall Sr. took his place in the partnership. Only thirty years old, Charles had barely started his circus career. His sister Ida Blair (1861–1894) had died the year before of Bright's disease; thus George Sr. had lost two of his four children in consecutive years.

Jessie Hall remained on the McFlinn and Hall show through its closing in May 1898. We do not find her again until her appearance with Gollmar Brothers Circus of Baraboo in 1900. She was on the Lemen brothers' Pan-American Circus in 1904 and on Adam Forepaugh & Sells Bros. Circus in 1905. Her marriage to Frank Macart had ended by then, and she married Walter Gollmar, one of the circus-owning brothers. Their son, Walter Jr., supplied much of what we know of his mother's career.

Jessie's circus life had begun when she was three years old and appeared in an illusion act in her father's sideshow. She later became a wirewalker and trapeze performer before turning to her specialty of handling snakes. Her mother, under the name Zula Zangara, had been a snake handler before her and must have handed on her knowledge. Jessie used the name Ilma when before the public. Sarah Wilder Hall had also appeared in tiger acts, but that occupation was spared her daughter. Jessie retired from performing when she married Gollmar.

The turn of the century found the Hall family thoroughly engaged in outdoor amusements. Popcorn had his Col. G. W. Hall's Circus and Menagerie, a wagon show. George W. Hall Jr.'s Circus and Menagerie was also a wagon show. In 1902 George Jr. called his outfit G. W. Hall & Son's Circus as his boys, Frank E. (1883–1936) and Charles (1897–1956), had joined him. The latter is usually referred to as Charles Russell to distinguish him from his uncle Charles, who had died in 1896.

Hall Sr. and his second wife, Mary Louise—called Lou—had one child, a daughter, Mabel, born in 1875. Under her father's tutelage, Mabel became a very competent horse trainer, and later (in 1900) took on the training and exhibition of her father's elephant, Columbus.

Mabel Hall was considered to be the only female elephant trainer of her day and one of the few women to ever undertake that very difficult profession. Among her charges was a brutish male tusker, Charlie (a.k.a. Columbus, Jumbo II, and Rajah), one of the most dangerous in the business. Cabinet photograph, undated, courtesy Eager Free Public Library, Evansville, Wisconsin.

This was a large beast, and to see him put through his routine by a woman was an unusual and popular act. In 1908 her father acquired another big elephant, Charlie, and Mabel took on his exhibition. As we said previously, Mabel was with her father's 1896 circus. She exhibited Charlie and a group of leopards trained by George Sr. on the Hargreaves Circus of Chester, Pennsylvania, for the seasons of 1904 to 1907. She married the treasurer of the show, Frank Longbotham, in 1905. They were divorced, and she married William P. Campbell. In 1915 William put out the New Orleans Minstrels with the help of his new father-in-law. This two-car railroad company occupied the couple until 1919, when they changed it to The Hall Shows, which was more of a circus than the vaudeville-type of show they had been operating. Through all of these changes Mary Louise Hall had traveled with Mabel. She did this until her death in 1923 in Murphy, Tennessee.

So imbued with the circus and its career possibilities were George Jr.'s children, Popcorn's grandchildren, that they too chose it as a life's work. Their efforts maintained Evansville's role as a show town.

Frank E. Hall (1883–1936) is first found with his father's G. W. Hall Jr.'s Trained Animal Show in 1894. When we speak of his being with the circus, we refer to his being listed in publicity. In actuality, he probably tagged along from the time he could walk. Since his mother, and most circus wives, for that matter, went with the troupe, the children did as well. One exception to this was Jessie Hall Macart's children, Vivian and Fred, who returned to Evansville when school started each fall. Walter Gollmar Jr., on the other hand, tells of splitting his school year between Evansville and Baraboo. He would begin each fall in Evansville and switch to Baraboo when the family moved there each spring to participate in the preparations for the Gollmar Bros.' Circus season.

Frank Hall framed an animal sideshow, à la "Popcorn George" Hall, in 1907 and traveled with the Great Melbourne Show, owned by the Wintermute brothers of Hebron, Wisconsin. In 1912 he married Zella Wintermute and in 1913 became a partner with his brother-in-law in the Wintermute & Hall Circus. This lasted through 1917, when the show was disbanded. In 1919 and 1920 the Col. George W. Hall Circus title was resurrected by Frank and his aunt Mabel's husband, William P. Campbell.

Confusion reigned in 1923 and 1924 when both Frank and his brother, Charles Russell Hall, put out competing companies, both named Hall Bros. Show. Frank changed his title to Vanderburg Bros. Circus in 1926, the name he operated under until his death in 1936. His wife, Zella, continued to operate Vanderburg Bros. until 1938.

We come now to Grace Hall (1886–1963), the only daughter of George Hall Jr. She performed as "Little Gracie" on her father's circus beginning in 1896. As a five-year-old, she han-

The Hall family members were all well-schooled in the training and handling of animals. Here Frank E. Hall, a third generation Hall, presents a mixed act of various breeds of dogs and a pony. Note the stake and rope enclosure circling the ring. Photograph, 1917, Zella Wintermute Hall Gift, Circus World Museum.

dled snakes in the sideshow as well as appearing on the trapeze in the arena. She married Howard A. Bruce in 1911, and in 1914 they started the H. A. Bruce Circus, which they operated until 1935. The Bruce company, a small wagon show that was later mounted on eight trucks, became a motion-picture-projection outfit in 1929. They visited the smallest of towns showing popular movies.

Charles Russell Hall (1897–1956), George Hall Jr.'s third child, under his father's tutelage specialized in wild-animal training and presentation. As we said earlier, he had Hall Bros. Show in 1923 and 1924. Charles R. Hall's Trained Animal Show was his usual title, in some years as a separate attraction, in others as an adjunct to larger circuses. He persevered until the 1950s and was the last of the Hall family to tour.

Begun in 1848 on Nathan Howes's New York Circus, the saga of the Hall family in the outdoor entertainment business lasted just over one hundred years and throughout four generations. Its Evansville sojourn began with the 1881 season, when Popcorn Hall first took his show out of new winter quarters. It had not ended at this writing since a courtly gentleman, Walter Gollmar Jr., son of Jessie Hall, still resides in the town. If Evansville did not quite reach the fame of Delavan and Baraboo as a circus center, it was not through any failing of George Washington Hall and his progeny. The old showman started in business when the tents were lit by candlelight and progressed through naphtha, kerosene, gasoline, and electric lights. In a long interview in the *Chicago Tribune* in 1913, Popcorn related of a season in Iowa:

The Hall Family

You couldn't find a hotel in any of the places where we stopped. Just a sawmill and a house scattered here and there. Our womenfolks and children were lodged in a house of some kind overnight, but the men had to sleep under the wagons or anywhere else they could find, if they slept at all. We trailed under difficulties in those days, but we were a strong, robust lot of people because of it.

THE RINGLING BROTHERS

On September 7, 1869, John Stowe & Co.'s Western Circus appeared in McGregor, Iowa, a small Mississippi River town. Among the performers in this wagon show was a citizen of McGregor, Andrew Gaffney, the circus strongman. He was well-known and well-liked by his neighbors, especially some boys who were attending their first circus thanks to a family pass that Gaffney had given their father. They were Albert, Gus, Alf T., Otto, Charles, and John Ringling, and over the next sixty-five years they were to see many circus performances, mostly their own. But of that first performance Alf T. Ringling later wrote:

It was an old-fashioned one-ring show … to the Ringling youngsters it stood out then, and stands out today as the greatest show, the brightest and most delightful that ever was given.

He went on to say that the performance that day inspired the boys to "first talk circus among themselves." He must have been speaking of Al, who was then seventeen, and Gus, fifteen, as the others were too young for such dreams, Otto being but eleven and John four.

Other than the name Barnum, there is no more famous American circus name than Ringling. For the past eighty years the Ringling Brothers name has been combined with Barnum and Bailey to create "The Greatest Show on Earth." Prior to 1919, however, they were separate entities, with quite different histories. And their individual stories are contrasts in the methodology of building corporate greatness. Barnum's show, as we've discussed in the chapter on W. C. Coup, literally emerged full-grown by the combination of money and astute business acumen. The Ringling brothers, on the other hand, achieved success one step at a time, growing from a tiny hall show to a great enterprise through the perseverance of the five remarkable siblings. Theirs was a story that could be brought to fruition only in America, with its wide-open spaces and burgeoning cities. This country provided enough space and people to enrich five showmen who started out

It's March or April and the snow is still on the ground in Ringlingville, the area along Water Street in Baraboo where the Ringling circus winter quarters were located. The repaired and newly painted baggage wagons and cages are spotted on the street, ready to be loaded for the annual tour. Photograph, circa 1905, Baraboo, Wisconsin, Mrs. Milton Leisman Gift, Circus World Museum.

dancing on a stage and ended up with the greatest show business empire that ever existed. And only in America could they have done this by bringing to the public the exotic and the bizarre.

They were the sons of August and Marie Salome Ringling. August was an often struggling harness maker who moved from town to town in an effort to improve his lot and provide for his eight children. McGregor, Iowa, was but one stop on the family journey. Chicago and Milwaukee, Prairie du Chien, Baraboo, and Rice Lake, Wisconsin, were others. It was in Baraboo that the Ringling circus was born, and as with Delavan, Janesville, and Evansville, the presence of a circus winter quarters carried this rural village into not only Wisconsin's pantheon, but that of the nation at large.

Al Ringling seems to have started it all by becoming involved in performing in 1879 as a juggler and acrobat when he was not working as a carriage trimmer. He appeared with and even managed small concert companies prior to the formation of the brothers' own such organization. As the oldest and most experienced of the family, Al must be given credit for the impetus toward show business that the others followed.

In 1882, Al came home to Baraboo from Brodhead, Wisconsin, and, according to a hypothesis by J. J. Schlicter, convinced brothers Alf T. and Charles to organize Ringling Brothers' Classic and Comic Concert Company. This was a hall show, given in small-town opera houses and featuring instrumental music, comic skits, and acrobatics. They first performed on November 27 in Mazomanie, Wisconsin.

"Stage fright" is the term that describes what happened to them on that memorable occasion, as they stumbled into each other, made miscues on their instruments, and were generally unable to mirror the professionalism they thought their rehearsals had indicated. Their audience of about fifty people constituted a thirteen-dollar house and took it all in stride.

The brothers continued offering their hall shows until the spring of 1884, by which time they had amassed ten or twelve hundred dollars and reached a decision to launch a circus. They hired the old showman Yankee Robinson (1818–1884) to be the ostensible manager and titled this first effort Yankee Robinson and Ringling Brothers Great Double Shows. They played their opening date on May 19 in Baraboo, in a yard adjacent to the jail. The names on that historic roster were published by the *New York Clipper* and read as follows:

Ed Boyd, press agent; Samuel McKenzie, bill poster; W. H. (Otto) Ringling, treasurer; Alf Ringling, band leader; Charles Ringling, leader of orchestra; nine men in band and orchestra; Al Ringling, equestrian manager; W. E. DeNar, museum superintendent; Tom Morton, canvas; Frank Seman, boss hostler.

Clowns: John Ringling and A. E. Pierce.

Company: A. W. Fox, Al Ringling, P. H. Daly, F. H. Sparks, Will Stuart, A. Parson, John Ringling, Will Gunkel, Mlle. Julie Carter, Madame Blanche.

Concert: six persons.

Other than in 1884, the Ringling name never appeared in a secondary position in any circus title. Handbills like this one, called "heralds" in circus parlance, were distributed in large quantities a few weeks in advance of the arrival of the circus. Herald, 1884, courtesy John and Mable Ringling Museum of Art, Sarasota, Florida.

Sideshow: George W. Hall, Jr. Attractions: educated hog, headless rooster, Circassian lady, electric lady, magician and fire king, Indian box mystery, and happy family.

Candy privilege: P. F. Baker & Co.

There were thirty horses (most of them hired), one trick horse, twelve wagons, four tents, and thirty-five workmen.

These were the first of thousands of people who followed the Ringling banner over the years. The constant, of course, were the five, later seven, Ringling brothers themselves. They were seven dedicated men who must have seemed like an avalanche to their competitors. Richard Ringling, Charles's son, was quoted, "Perhaps it wasn't that the uncles were so smart, but that there were so God-damned many of them." They came to decisions in parley and worked as one mind when the path was decided upon. They had arguments galore but closed ranks once policy was chosen. This was their manner throughout the more than forty years of their circus proprietorship, that is, until the death of Charles in 1926 left only John at the helm.

In correspondence with third parties they did not sign their individual names but ended letters with "Ringling Brothers." No rival had as many competent managers or as much unsupervised talent.

"While at first we were jacks-of-all-trades," John Ringling wrote, "able to do almost anything, from leading the band to doing an equestrian act, it became necessary to specialize and divide the work. We were some time adjusting ourselves, and learning which of us was best fitted for certain departments."

Once they had parceled out the various tasks, the brothers each ran his own fief, and unless asked for advice they did not interfere in one another's decisions. In addition, there was never a written contract between them, and they shared equally in the profits. A clerk in their Baraboo bank said that an express company delivered the cash from the show to the bank every day, and it was divided into five portions, one to each brother's account.

There has been almost as much written about the Ringlings as about P. T. Barnum, and as with Barnum, there is a certain amount of hyperbole in the various accounts. One leaves the accumulation wishing for a few negatives, but they are not present in any number. If the

More than any other image, the overlapping profiles of the five Ringling brothers symbolized the World's Greatest Shows and its family values. Left to right, the brothers are Alf T., Al, John, Otto, and Charles. The arrangement was first employed in 1893. Courier, 1894, Dr. H. H. Conley Gift, Circus World Museum.

circus was a religion, the Ringling saga would be its *Lives of the Saints*. But they were no saints. Charles and John were skirt chasers; Henry had a drinking problem until the others sat on him. These were the better-known sins among them.

It is unfortunate that most commentators lump the brothers together, excepting John, who has been the subject of several biographies. This came about because of John's tremendous accumulation of wealth, always a fascinating subject, but it may also indicate that the drama of their lives occurred mainly in the circus ring and in the events that propelled them to the very zenith of field show operations.

In order to emphasize their individuality, we will present each brother in turn, with the comments made by the various chroniclers who have observed or researched their careers.

AL (Albrecht C. Ringling, 1852–1916)

Al was the leader, the brother most dedicated to the idea of perfection in their art. He was "Mr. Circus." A highly nervous man, sharp-eyed and quick moving, he lived for the show and worked unceasingly to improve it. He began his public life as a juggler (called a "balancer" in nineteenth-century usage). His most-often-mentioned early accomplishment was his ability to balance a sod-breaking plow on his chin. Early on he was listed as proprietor and manager in the advertisements, while his brothers were still undecided as to who would do what. He settled into the role of equestrian director, that is, the man responsible for the program and the hiring of performers. Brother John once wrote that Al was the greatest producing showman the world had known. "He knew instinctively what the public would like." That is probably an overstatement, considering that a comparison to Barnum, James Bailey, Adam Forepaugh, and men of that ilk must be included, but it is a tribute nonetheless to Al's ability to produce interesting and exciting content. His title for many years was "Director of Exhibitions," as he organized and produced the great spectacles that were a part of circus presentations of the day. These had large casts, not all of them ring performers, in such costume dramas as "The Crusaders," "Joan of Arc," and "Solomon and the Queen of Sheba." The pantomime dramas opened the performance, and the hippodrome races closed them.

Al had a most retentive memory; he remembered the help he received from sympathetic friends, indulgent landlords, and liverymen whom he was sometimes unable to pay in the early years. When the show finally reached a level of success, he paid those bills with interest. Charles Ringling wrote that Al was the brother who was always before the public—in the performance, in the parade, and on the show grounds. The others, because of their separate duties, were seldom seen, except by the employees. It sounds as if he was a driven man, yet his nephew, Henry Ringling North, said Al had the sweetest disposition of all the brothers. He rarely joked, and he didn't countenance vulgarity. It was his favorite remark, when asked to explain the brothers' success, to reply, "We had a little money, and a lot of gall, and made good." He was an adult-onset diabetic and died after a two-year retirement.

OTTO (William Henry Ringling, 1858–1911)

The most well-read of the clan and the owner of a large library, Otto Ringling never married; he lived with brother Alf T. and his wife after they built a large Baraboo home. His main interests were horses, books, and mathematics. He was the treasurer of the company and one of the leaders in business decisions involving expenditure. It was to him that the other brothers turned when they were short of money, as he always seemed to have some. He appears to have been very level-headed, very quiet, and very methodical. The brothers called him "The King" because he wielded the power of the purse at all times. He was penurious in small matters, but Wild West showman Gordon Lillie called him "the biggest man I ever dealt with" after Lillie negotiated the purchase of the Buffalo Bill equipment with him. Otto had the fiscal equivalent of Al's knack for programming. In 1903 he suggested that the brothers acquire fifteen-acre plots in the central area of all the large cities they played, since show lots were becoming difficult to find. Such prescience was beyond the thinking of the others, and Otto was voted down. He and John urged the purchase of Barnum & Bailey from Bailey's widow in 1907 right in the face of a financial panic. When they bought their rival, it was Otto who was sent to Bridgeport, Connecticut, to evaluate the property. His letter to the brothers outlining a scheme of what to use and what to discard clearly indicates that his knowledge of the business was not confined to balancing the books. And it was Otto's taking over the management of the new acquisition that put the show back in the profitable column it had enjoyed under James A. Bailey. Otto shared with brother John the virtue of being the most farsighted of the family.

In addition to his love of books, Otto had a love of food—all the Ringlings tended toward corpulence—that nephew Henry North thought led to his early demise. Al's diabetes was probably a manifestation of the same tendency. However, John, whose appetite was enormous, lived to be seventy. Otto, dead at fifty-three, was the only one of the brothers who was born in Baraboo. His funeral was held in Al Ringling's mansion, across the street from the very modest home in which he had been born. In a letter attached to his will he wrote, "We have labored together successfully a long time. Goodbye."

ALF T. (Alfred Theodore Ringling, 1863–1919)

The leading wordsmith among the brothers, Alf T. also played several instruments, including the cornet, on which he soloed in the wagon-show days. He sang, juggled, and contributed an Irish impression, this last in the concert or after-show. He was the superintendent of the sideshow and was its lecturer as well as the director of the press department in the early years. Later, he concentrated on the advertising. "He loved words and the people who wrote them," his niece said of him. Beginning in 1895, it was Alf T. who wrote the annual route books, those seasons' histories that were provided to the employees and are of inestimable value to researchers. His 1900 book, *Life Story of the Ringling Brothers*, is another fine source of the family progress despite its advocative bent. Couriers, newspaper-like advertisements that were broadcast ahead of the show and had been introduced by P. T. Barnum in 1871, fell to

Alf T. to write, and these provide good examples of his way with words. No adjective seems to have avoided his pen. He once described a hyena as "The Mammoth, Marauding, Man-eating Monstrosity."

Another of the brothers to die young—he was fifty-six—Alf T. lived just long enough to see Ringling Brothers and Barnum & Bailey open at Madison Square Garden in New York City in 1919, the first year of the combination. Unfortunately, his death left only John and Charles to head the firm, and their rivalry, always simmering just beneath the surface, became obvious to those around them.

CHARLES (Carl Edward Ringling, 1864–1926)

The most musically talented of the family, Charles presented duets with Alf T. on violins as well as vocally, a euphonium solo, and a bass solo in the Concert Company days. In the first year of the circus, 1884, he sang alone and in duets and offered a trombone solo. In 1885 he performed in the concert, or after-show, doing sketches and songs. By 1886 his time was wholly taken up with advertising the troupe. It was he who saw to the posters while Alf T. wrote the copy for newspaper ads and the couriers and heralds. Charles was also responsible for dealing with the opposition, the attempts by other companies to interfere with Ringling advertising. This amounted to the defacing or covering of posted material and scurrilous ads demeaning the size and worth of the brothers' troupe. Beginning in 1916, on Al Ringling's death, Charles took over the production and direction of the great spectacles that began each performance.

Charles left an outline for a history of the brothers similar to but much more personal than the one published by Alf T. in 1900. It is a most interesting document, calling for much reading between the lines, since it was never put in finished form. The things that were important to him, assuming the book took the form he outlined, were often of a nostalgic nature. He planned to tell of his musical beginnings with Alf T. in Prothero's orchestra in Baraboo, he on the cornet and Alfred on the violin. They also joined in E. M. Kimball's musicales (Kimball was in the concert company in 1882 and 1883). His descriptions of McGregor, Iowa, show how much he relished the family's life in that tiny town. He seemed to be discomfited by the building of the railroad bridge across the Mississippi to Prairie du Chien because it doomed McGregor, which had been an important river port.

The boys' father had come over the bluffs by stagecoach from Sauk City when he moved to Baraboo in 1855, and Charles thought of that journey when the circus left Baraboo for the first time, in 1884, and took the same road to Sauk City. Their neighbors had predicted disaster for the circus, but one man, George Mertens, had confidence in them. Fortunately, Mertens was a Baraboo banker. The four brothers (John joined later in the season), in a buggy filled with Otto's books, followed grass trails. They often ate wild ducks, which they shot with revolvers.

Since he was in charge of advertising, Charles discussed P. T. Barnum, whom he thought of as a great man who understood and appreciated advertising, and whom he credited with originating the American advertising system. The difference between the methods of Barnum's time and those of the Ringlings was that Charles's staff people were aware of the production and tonnage of factories and mines and the seasons of agriculture. Whereas Coup and Barnum were attuned to population, the Ringlings went further, judging such things as summer resorts and wheat and cotton harvests.

Charles thought the moral conduct of circus people was equal to the average of the towners they entertained. An important observation that he planned to point out in his history was that the work was physical and made no call on the emotions.

Alice Ringling Coerper, Gus Ringling's daughter, thought Charles was the sharpest member of the family—very energetic and quite witty. Henry North preferred Charles's company to that of his Uncle John. A handsome man, and at five-foot-ten the smallest of the brothers, he was popular with the employees. Very neat, and always well-dressed, Charles would not tolerate slovenliness in his department.

The most surprising of Charles's observations was his ambivalence toward John Ringling. At one point he described his brother as "I - me - my," and at another as "the self advertiser." Writer Tom Parkinson quoted Charles describing John as "the perfect scrooge." This would seem to be something of a sibling rivalry; however, the records indicate no friction as far as the operation of the circus was concerned. Charles contrasted Al's popularity with that of John to John's detriment.

Charles planned to dedicate his memoir to Alf T. He wrote, "In my 60th year, when I hear a school bell I hasten my step with Alfred, and when I take my fiddle out, somehow I feel he is not far away."

Charles died in December 1926 of a heart ailment.

JOHN (John Nicholas Ringling, 1866–1936)

When he was nineteen years old (1885), John Ringling ceased his work as a clown and became the advance man for the show. John was once observed riding in a spring wagon behind two scraggly horses, dressed to the nines and going into Iowa to spread the word that the Ringling brothers were coming. Much of the rest of his life was taken up with routing the show. This required that he know the territory, the roads, the receptive towns, the possibility of rival interference, and, later, the railroad system and its many schedules and rates. His would seem to have been the most fascinating task of any of the brothers. There is an apocryphal story that John could put his hand out a train window and name the county he was passing through. Henry North described him as sticking a nail file in a *Consolidated Railway Guide* to within a page or two of any railroad timetable Henry might name. If these stories are not true, they at least explain the aura surrounding John Ringling's expertise.

John was his mother's favorite, his niece wrote, a brilliant man with a phenomenal memory. He could recite extemporaneously the railway path from any place to any other, by line and junction, it has been said. Tall, curly-haired, and handsome, John was a ladies' man, even after he married. Baraboo was too small for him (he referred to its citizens as Baraboobians), and he left as soon as he could afford to. For some years he lived in Chicago, then later in New York. A true metropolitan, impeccably dressed, he nevertheless adopted a country-boy image in his business dealings, passing himself off as a hick from Wisconsin. He often scheduled business meetings for late evening, feeling that his conferees would be tired after a day's work and not as sharp-minded as he, who hadn't risen until noon.

Though he amassed a large fortune, John never veered from his duties as one of the partners. When he and Charles were hugely rich and had no need for the concerns involved in managing the show, they couldn't bring themselves to sell it. "Mr. John" came to personify circus, as did P. T. Barnum and James Bailey before him.

So they proceeded, with John deciding where to go, Al arranging what would be shown, Alf T. writing the advertising, Charles keeping an eye on the competition, and Otto counting the money. These were the five who eventually ruled the American circus scene, but three other family members were intimately involved in their success.

GUS (Augustus Albert Ringling, 1854–1907)

Gus, the second son, did not participate in the family business until 1890, the year the circus went on the railroads. He left home as a young man and set up in business in Minneapolis, but was induced to join the others once their success was reasonably assured. He was not admitted to partnership; there is no record that he resented that fact. He took over the advance brigade, traveling ahead of the show and seeing to the placement of the advertising material on the barns and fences across the country. At first he had but two advance cars, and this eventually grew to encompass four. Though Charles Ringling led the "opposition" forces, it was Gus's troops who supplied the manpower for these "billing wars."

He was the gentlest of the brood, well-read, master of several languages, a bit of a dreamer. An outdoorsman with an affinity for animals, he has been described as having a "dreamy, poetic face." It is not what one would think of as a description of a hard-boiled circus advance man. As with Henry Ringling, Gus died in his fifties.

Henry Ringling did not become a Ringling Bros. partner until his brother Otto died in 1911. Though his size and countenance scared some, Henry was a gentle and cultivated man with a large personal library. Photograph, 1897, Circus World Museum.

HENRY (Henry William George Ringling, 1868–1918)

No commentator speaks of Henry Ringling without mentioning his size. At six-foot-three and 300 pounds, he was the giant of the family. As the youngest son, he was still in high school when his five brothers took out the Concert Company. He joined the troupe in 1886, the third year of the original wagon circus. It was decided to have him travel ahead of the show to map out the parade route for each town they were to visit. He was outfitted with a fine buggy, two handsome trotting horses, and a new wardrobe, so as to present a good image to the local townspeople. It proved too much for the eighteen-year-old village lad. He went on a drunken spree, sold the equipment and the fine clothes when his money gave out, and was found in a distressful state in a small Iowa town. His brothers forgave him and put him under their watch as superintendent of the main entrance to the big top. Eventually, Henry stopped drinking altogether, but not before he suffered mightily from remorse. In 1892 he took on the additional task of directing the concert. He was "morose and withdrawn" for the rest of his life, Henry North wrote, describing him as beetle-browed and sinister-appearing. When Otto died, he left his fifth of the circus to Henry. With the acquisition of the Adam Forepaugh & Sells Brothers show in 1905, Henry became its manager. He died on Armistice Day in 1918.

The Ringling wives, with two exceptions, took no part in the business, as would be expected in nineteenth-century families. They traveled on the trains but didn't necessarily enjoy it. When Alf T.'s wife divorced him in 1913, included in her bill of complaint was a statement that she had to accompany him on the road, which she never did voluntarily. Charles's wife, Edith Conway, participated for a short time after their marriage in 1899.

A real trouper at heart, Lou Ringling rode a horse in parade, charmed the snakes in the sideshow, presented an equestrian act in the big show, and directed the wardrobe preparations in the off-season. She is supposed to have remarked later of her highly regarded husband, Al, that when he got rich he got boring. Cabinet photograph, circa 1887, Howard Gusler Collection, Circus World Museum.

LOUISE (Eliza Morris Ringling, 1851–1941)

"Lou," as she was known, married Al Ringling in 1880 and was a bona fide member of the early wagon show. A very attractive woman, small and feisty, she determined to do whatever it took to help her husband succeed. They were the first married couple in the brothers' generation, and Lou cooked for all of them when the boys were in Baraboo. She was a manège rider (sidesaddle, known as *haute école*) and a snake charmer. She and Jessie Hall Gollmar, who also handled snakes, were great friends. The story is told of her driving three wagons and a four-horse hitch for four days from Missouri to Baraboo, 350 miles, when some teamsters quit in 1887. She designed and sewed many of the early costumes and established the show's wardrobe shop in a Baraboo building.

The steady acquisition of equipment, horses, and wild animals, and the tale of the ever-increasing tent sizes, has been recorded many times, but less attention has been paid to the brothers' operating principles. First and foremost among these was fiscal conservatism. Their first tent was purchased secondhand from Dr. Morrison, who had a small 1879 circus of which Al Ringling had been a member. The brothers furnished the tent by going into the woods and cutting and peeling tamarack trees for poles, and sawing seatboards themselves. Charles pointed out that they never paid for sleeping car berths on the road, but sat up in day coaches. Otto's tight hand on the funds dictated that they pour every cent back into the show. Other equipment came from Joe Parson, whose Darlington, Wisconsin, circus, also graced by Al, had closed. Parson himself was with the Ringlings for several seasons as a performer.

When they constructed the barns for winter quarters, beginning in 1886, they left them unpainted, and no sign appeared saying what was in them. John M. Kelley, attorney for the circus, once wrote, "No Ringling ever took his hand off a dollar bill unless he could put his foot on it." Ostentation was not their forte.

In a time when most circuses, especially small ones that tried to garner every nickel they could, allowed "grift," shortchanging and crooked gaming devices, only a few managers were able to resist the temptations of the con men. Bailey, Barnum, and Coup were among these, but they were the giants of the trade. For a little show such as the Ringlings operated, to resist those blandishments was almost heresy. Charles Ringling said, "I recall that in the profession they used to call us 'The Sunday School boys,' because we eliminated the grafters (or grifters, as one pleases), and refused to let them travel in our wake. ... our success, I firmly believe, came from our recognition of the rights of the public by doing away with the many impositions that had been practiced against it. There was no shortchanging at the windows of our ticket wagons. We advertised exactly what we had. We discountenanced the presence of crooks, and cooperated with the local authorities in their prosecution ... It took time, but even-

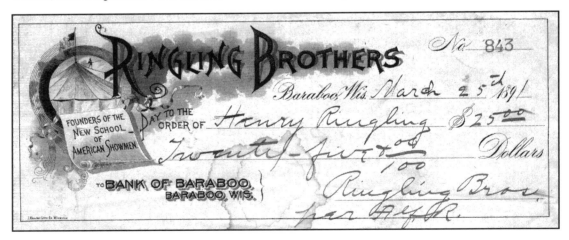

The derisive moniker "Sunday School show" originated with the Ringlings' 1891 adoption of the "Founders of the New School of American Showmen" slogan on their checks and in their advertising materials. The brothers had a long and mutually beneficial relationship with the Bank of Baraboo, which prospers today as The Baraboo National Bank. Check, 1891, courtesy Brad and Melissa Hintz.

tually the people of the country came to realize that our coming to town was not a grand rally of confidence men, and worse."

A newspaper comment in 1894 verified that the Ringlings had what was termed a "Sunday School Show," though the term must have predated that year. No profanity was allowed on the grounds, and no hangers-on (meaning grifters) were permitted for even a moment. It was described as the cleanest show that travels. They sought to set a moral tone, to create an aura of respectability, something often lacking in western circuses. By 1891 their printed material identified them as founding "The New School of American Showmen."

One of their chief rivals before 1905, Ben Wallace of Peru, Indiana, was so addicted to grift on his lots that he lost a partner in his Great Wallace Shows. For two seasons he had to

change the name of his circus until his audience forgot his previous depredations. Despite his proclivities, he made a fortune in the business, it must be noted.

The Ringlings could have done the same, but just as the Hollands, W. C. Coup, and Burr Robbins did, they chose the higher path. And it paid, not only in the manner of their reception, but in the type of employees they attracted. John Ringling claimed, in the *American Magazine*, "We discovered that we were getting a better class of workers, more loyalty from them, and better work and appearance. Also, we discovered that we were welcome to play return engagements, and that our reputation for honesty made us welcome."

This is a quintessential "Circus Day" in Iowa, a sultry afternoon with the breeze lifting the flags, the banners filled out by the wind and the tent canvas flapping with each gust. The crowd at the "front door" of the Ringling circus is observing Joe Parson walk a rope stretched over the big top. Card photograph, June 12, 1888, Algona, Iowa, F. M. Jones Gift, Circus World Museum.

The brothers, truth be told, were not innovators in any sense of presenting acts that were different from other circuses. As their show grew in profitability, they added higher-salaried performers, and more of them. This was very much in line with the history of the institution, which, as we quoted the words of W. C. Coup, had not changed in content, only in magnitude since its eighteenth-century beginning. The differences between what one saw in the Ringling tent compared to that of their rivals was mainly in the names of the artists. The actual differences are usually spelled out only in the minutiae revered by researchers. The advertising was as verbose, the street parade as grand, the tented city as large on one leading show as on another. But by setting the moral tone as they did, the brothers from Baraboo created an aura of respectability, throughout Wisconsin and the West.

As might be expected, the wagon-borne Ringling circus confined itself to what we now call the Midwest. And since population is the key to circus movement, they chose to spend

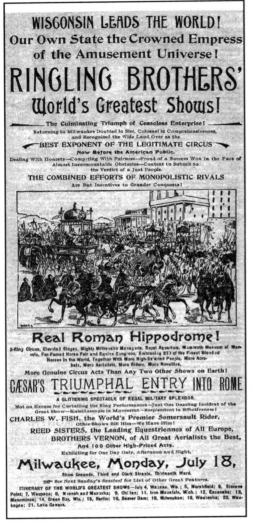

Engaged in a competitive war with the much larger Barnum & Bailey Greatest Show on Earth (28 cars versus 64 cars), the Ringlings proudly proclaimed their Wisconsin origins and the state's status when the battle was taken into Milwaukee. Written hyperbole with slight mention of the best features now fills the ads. Newspaper advertisement, 1892, Circus World Museum.

much time in Iowa. Here were a million and a half people in the 1880s, and at most, four cities of any size. The vast majority of Iowans were farmers, and the villages that the Ringlings visited were fifteen to twenty miles apart across flat fields. It was almost a perfect wagon-show environment. As had Orton and Burr Robbins before them, the Ringlings found that the prairie people welcomed them and their entertainment.

In 1884 the Ringlings spent sixty percent of the season in Iowa; in 1885, eighty percent; and in 1886, fifty-one percent. The remainder of their dates were in Wisconsin, Minnesota, and Illinois. In 1887 they discovered Nebraska, Kansas, and Missouri and evened out their visits between those states and Iowa. This trek to Nebraska was the only one to that area for the Ringlings.

They were not alone in their appreciation of Iowa, and competition was often a concern. This may be the reason they spent almost the entire season of 1889 in Illinois (eighty-five percent of their dates, with just twenty-one in Wisconsin). It will be recalled that Burr Robbins spent 1879 in Illinois and had one of his best seasons.

In the fall of 1889 Otto and John Ringling went to Philadelphia and purchased eleven railroad cars from Adam Forepaugh. Later, they acquired more cars from Thomas Grenier, the man who bought out Burr Robbins. The brothers had decided that they would become a railroad circus in 1890. This was a big step, as the rituals of overland circus operation were much different from those of railroading. Not only was the equipment expensive, but the outlay for transportation had to be paid in advance. A wagon show had only to reach the first stand with but license and lot rental to be paid before ticket sales were received. The added expense of the train crew made the railroad show payroll a burden if the exchequer was thin after the expense of wintering the company. The greatest advantage, as Coup and Barnum had proven twenty years before, was that a railroad show could avoid the smaller places and visit only larger towns that promised more ticket buyers.

Freed from the slow pace of the wagon show, one would expect John Ringling's 1890 route to expand the company's horizons. Instead, he returned to Iowa, but was able, with the new system, to cover most of the state, using nine weeks to do so. Prior to going on rails the Ringlings would visit about a quarter of the state in the same time. After Iowa the next five weeks were spent in Wisconsin, then after three weeks in Ohio, they went into Pennsylvania, as far east as they'd ever been. They turned south at Indiana, Pennsylvania, touched Maryland and West Virginia, and headed toward home. They played mostly in towns whose populations were 2,500 to 5,000, but in 1890 John Ringling routed them into thirteen cities with populations over 10,000. He had never done this when they traveled by wagon. In 1891, he increased this figure to twenty-five cities, including Milwaukee for the first time.

Going so far east in 1890 was like throwing a spear at Barnum & Bailey and other big eastern circuses. It was a forerunner of future depredations. The Ringlings seemed to be announcing that they were no longer a little western show. They gradually increased the size of their train, going from eighteen cars in 1890 to fifty in 1896 and sixty-five in 1903. By so doing they opened themselves up to the competitive skirmishes in which the larger shows engaged. Opposition, in the form of billing wars (Charles Ringling called them "sticker wars"), wherein competing crews worked furiously for space for their lithographs, were expensive.

In 1892, the Ringlings had confrontations with Barnum & Bailey in Kansas City and Topeka, and when they reached Milwaukee the two entities were nearly at knifepoint. The Ringling brothers were in the city on July 18, Barnum & Bailey on August 15. "Milwaukee was turned into a rosy picture gallery," the *New York Clipper* announced, "and every available awning, streetcar, dry goods box, and loafer's lounging place was plastered, replastered, and shin plastered with eloquent red, blue and green." Tempers flared and there were several conflicts, but little paper was destroyed. However, James Bailey sued the brothers in Milwaukee for their actions against his billposters. The Ringlings countersued for libel, claiming they were injured by handbills published by the larger show. Both actions were subsequently withdrawn.

A large bill stand featuring Ringling portraits serves as a backdrop to the passage of a Ringling icon. The musical bell wagon was built by the Moellers in Baraboo, relatives of the Ringlings, with carvings and bells crafted in Milwaukee. It still survives in Ringling show ownership, on loan to Circus World Museum. Card photograph, August 17, 1892, Black River Falls, Wisconsin, Circus World Museum.

One of the claims Bailey's advertisements made was that this "small show" (meaning Ringling Bros.) had not played Chicago, New York, Philadelphia, Baltimore, St. Louis, and Cincinnati because "their inferiority would be so disastrously apparent."

In 1894 the Sells Brothers Circus launched a campaign in Texas in which they called the Ringlings "The Ananias Brothers from Bugaboo, the World's Greatest Dodgers." They offered "A word of advice to fresh young fellows," which was "Don't try to lie your way through the world." The Ananias name was lifted from a Biblical verse.

Adam Forepaugh & Sells' Brothers in 1896 referred to "The Ding-dong Bros. Circus from Bugaboo" in describing their meetings in Ohio, Indiana, and Iowa. In one place, Charles

Ringling concealed himself and some of his helpers in order to keep an eye on a particularly good spread of their paper. When an opposition crew appeared, the Ringling forces attacked and drove them off.

As their show grew in size from year to year, the Ringling routes were expanded to cover more of the cities. They made their first visit to Detroit in 1893, to Texas in 1894, to Boston in 1895, and to Houston in 1896. All of these places were considered by one show or another as their "territory." Sells Brothers, for instance, had been going to Texas for fifteen years and treated that fact as if it granted a sort of primogeniture among larger circuses.

Facing the reality that competition was expensive and wasteful, various companies entered into collusive agreements that allocated certain territories to each other. James A. Bailey and the Ringling Brothers reached such an agreement in 1894 by which certain towns in the Midwest would not be played by one of them until the other had first appeared there. However, a similar agreement between Bailey and the Sells Brothers in 1894 was quickly abrogated by Bailey, according to Peter Sells.

The Ringling menagerie was the most extensive traveling aggregation of wild beasts to be seen anywhere during its heyday. Numerous cages housed a variety of mammals, with lead stock, like camels, tethered along picket lines in the middle of the menagerie. Every big top customer passed through the animals before seeing the big show. Photograph, 1910, Circus World Museum.

It was Bailey's desire to take his circus to England and the Continent, which he did in December 1897. He bought the Great Adam Forepaugh Show from the founder's estate in 1890 and combined it with the Sells Brothers' Circus in 1896 to form Adam Forepaugh and Sells Brothers America's Greatest Shows Consolidated. He installed the Sells brothers as managers. Part of his reasoning would seem to be to provide competition for the Ringlings, B. E. Wallace, and John Robinson while Barnum & Bailey spent four years abroad. What actually transpired was that, freed of any competition from Barnum & Bailey, the Ringlings were able to roam the country like a car of juggernaut, establishing their name in places they'd never been. Additionally, the Ringlings leased the John Robinson Circus in 1898 and operated two large companies in that season.

They went into the Pacific Northwest in 1899 and 1900 and into California in 1900 and 1902. When Barnum & Bailey returned to America in 1903, Bailey embarked on a great building program, having the Sebastian Wagon Company create an enormous parade with which he hoped to reestablish his show's ascendancy. Instead, the new properties proved so unwieldy that Bailey gave up the street parade for two seasons. In other words, he abandoned the greatest advertising specialty that circuses had.

In 1905, Bailey sold half of the Forepaugh–Sells show to the Ringlings. Bailey died in April 1906, and the Ringling brothers promptly bought the other half from Mrs. Bailey. Henry

The mammoth size of the Ringling Bros. tent city at its zenith can be appreciated in this hillside view. All of the apparatus was transported, unloaded, erected, utilized, taken down, and shipped to the next city within a twenty-four hour period, six days a week. Additionally, a street parade, two big top shows, two band concerts, and sideshow and menagerie operations were staged during the day, along with feeding and transporting 1,200 people and entertaining up to 12,000 people at a single performance. Photograph, August 31, 1915, Red Wing, Minnesota, Steve Albasing Gift, Circus World Museum.

Ringling became the manager of Forepaugh–Sells. They prepared to purchase the Carl Hagenbeck circus in 1906, but dropped the idea. In 1907 the brothers bought the Barnum & Bailey Circus (which included the equipment of the Buffalo Bill Wild West Show). Otto and John Ringling became the managers of the new acquisition. The Ringlings were then the circus kings of America.

True to their operating formula, the brothers decided to purchase the Barnum & Bailey Circus by a family plebiscite. Otto and John were in favor of it. The others opposed it at first, feeling that they did not have the manpower necessary to operate three large troupes. This question was solved by retiring the Forepaugh–Sells Circus and splitting the country between Barnum & Bailey and Ringling Brothers.

For the next ten years, the two big shows were operated separately, Ringling from Baraboo and Barnum & Bailey from Bridgeport, Connecticut. The Buffalo Bill equipment was sold to Pawnee Bill in 1909. The Forepaugh–Sells title was revived in 1910 and 1911, under Al Ringling's guidance.

By the time of Otto's death in 1911, the brothers were financially secure and as interested in investing and spending their fortunes as they were in overseeing the day-to-day operation of the empire they had created. Only Al Ringling still lived in Baraboo; the others had mansions in various parts of the country. Charles was in Evanston, John in New York, Alf T. in New Jersey. Each of them visited the shows from time to time, but the organization they had built and the managers they had hired were perfectly capable of operating the enterprise.

Al Ringling died in 1916, further closing the circle, and in 1918 two decisions of importance were made. The first was to winter both shows in Bridgeport; later it was decided to combine the circuses. Thus came into being today's Ringling Brothers and Barnum & Bailey's Combined Shows. After thirty-four years in Baraboo, the Ringling circus left Wisconsin at the beginning of the 1918 season, never more to reside there.

The Ringlings had begun in the jail yard in Baraboo in 1884 and ended (as Ringling Brothers) in Waycross, Georgia, on October 8, 1918. Three of the original brothers were left, men who had danced on village stages and went on to create the greatest circus combine that the world had ever seen.

Rose Dockrill was one Delavan resident who achieved great fame for her ring virtuosity. A tribute to her star quality was the issuance of this special poster. Lithograph, 1897, Gordon Yadon Gift, Circus World Museum.

Herds of performing pachyderms doing precision drills and skits were typical on circuses at the turn of the century. The addition of a recognized breed of dogs made the Kassell-titled presentation by head elephant man George "Deafy" Denman noteworthy. Lithograph, 1910, Jos. Schlitz Brewing Company Gift, Circus World Museum.

The Ringling brothers were at the pinnacle of the circus business in 1909. Their combined portraits were a corporate logo recognized throughout the United States. Lithograph, 1909, courtesy Howard Tibbals.

Cows and other farm beasts were seldom trained for presentation in a circus ring. Two different Wisconsin circuses, including Burr Robbins, did provide such entertainment to the amazement of Midwestern agriculturalists. Lithograph, 1881, courtesy Howard Tibbals.

Similar to a 1916 Barnum & Bailey bill, this eye-catching poster also included a contemporary admonition for parents. The statement bears testimony to the devotion, and sound business principles, of the circus's owner. Poster, 1960, Marv Gauger Gift, Circus World Museum.

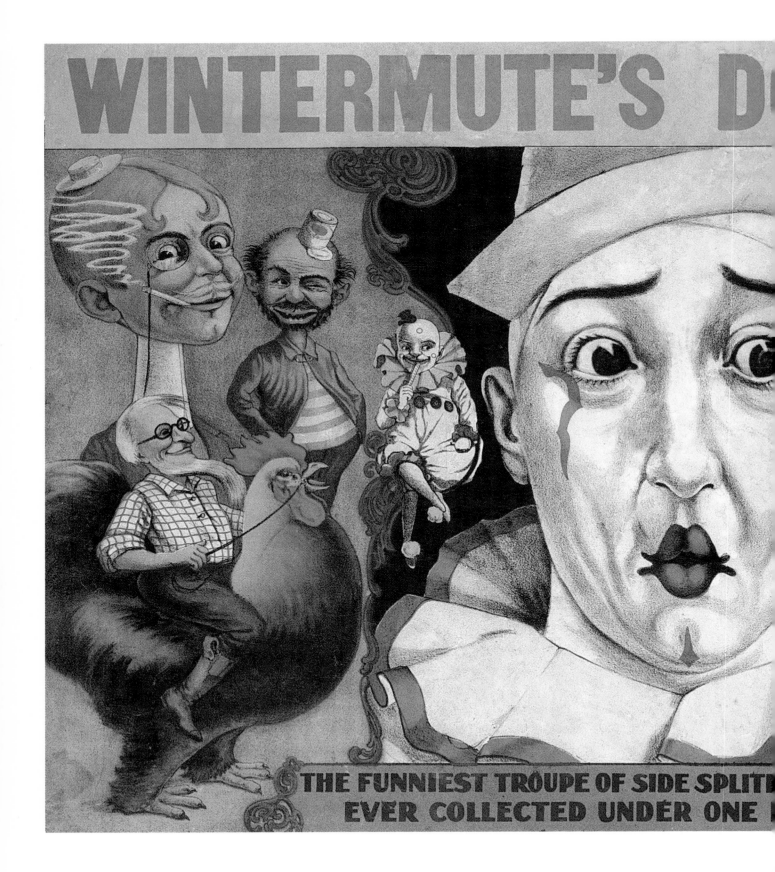

The pensive clown in this poster, so different from the usual merrymakers seen on typical circus posters, was sure to draw attention to the upcoming arrival of the Wintermute show. Lithograph, circa 1915, courtesy Stephen T. Flint.

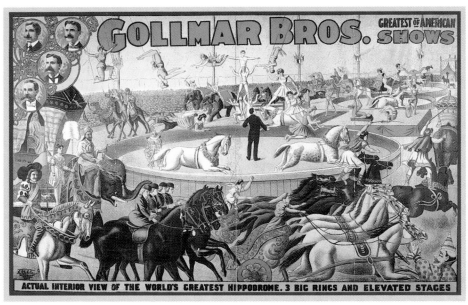

*The splendor and variety of a great circus performance
from the early twentieth century is captured in this
special piece of Gollmar Bros. paper. Lithograph, 1912,
Circus World Museum.*

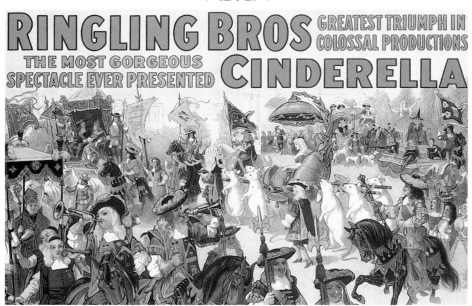

*Circus spectacles were an extra part of each Ringling circus
performance, with especially grand presentations in the
1910s. They brought to life epic events from history, fairy
tales, and other select themes. Lithograph, 1916,
Circus World Museum.*

A multitude of small animal acts were a staple of truck
shows in the 1930s. This is an example of stock paper that
could have been printed with any circus title on it.
Lithograph, 1936, Edna Curtis Christiansen Gift,
Circus World Museum.

With their unusual coloration and subject matter, the posters and window cards of the Fun on the Farm were as unique as the circus itself. Though contrived to advocate dairy interests, Kelley and Agee must have had considerable fun in staging their bovine-based entertainment. Lithograph, 1924, John M. Kelley Gift, Circus World Museum.

THE GOLLMAR BROTHERS

The newspapers in Baraboo were fascinated by the presence of the Ringling circus in their midst, reporting every move the brothers made from buying a llama to building a house. When another set of five brothers, the Gollmars, announced in November 1890 that they, too, were forming a show, *The Sauk County Democrat* predicted success. That only two of the Gollmars had any circus experience, and only a year's worth at that, was explained away thusly: "Since we enjoy their acquaintance, we cannot help stretching our imaginative powers." The newspaper went on to predict that the Ringlings and the Gollmars would take the place of Barnum and Forepaugh.

That a small village (5,000 people in 1890) could produce two circuses, even with a disparity of size between them, is a wonder itself, but that the two sets of owners were cousins is without parallel in circus history. They were related through the Juliar sisters, Salome being the mother of the Ringlings and Mary the mother of the Gollmars. There were actually eight sons in the Gollmar family, but only five were involved in their circus. And while there is no direct evidence that the Ringlings' success inspired their cousins, it must have been so.

Robert H. Gollmar, son of one of the brothers, wrote that after Christmas dinner in 1890, the men of the family first discussed the idea of forming a show. They already had a village band, made up of five Gollmars and three others, which they had formed some years before. The Ringlings were then in their ninth year as successful circus proprietors, surely an example of what could be accomplished.

Circus letterheads, and the envelopes that contained them, were embellished with finely executed graphics. The Gollmars (clockwise from top, Walt., B. F., Chas., and Fred C.) adopted a new subtitle, Greatest of American Shows, in 1905 and retained it through the final season of 1916. Letterhead, 1904, Circus World Museum.

The Gollmar Brothers

We must remember what the traveling circus promised to the young men of small towns in the nineteenth century. It was akin to the aspirations of actors or professional athletes of today. To the athletes among them, it provided an outlet for their energies; to the horsemen it held out a way to earn a living at what they liked to do; to the practical there were promises of reward that no farm or factory could match. And to all young men, it called with travel, adventure, and worldliness. To be a showman was to be somebody in that simpler time.

In order of their birth the Gollmars were Jacob C. (1851?–1896), Charles A. (1861–1929), Benjamin F. (1864–1947), Fred C. (1867–1965), and Walter S. (1869–1933). In 1890 Jacob was a blacksmith, Charles was a railroad machinist, Benjamin and Fred owned a furniture store (which in those days meant being an undertaker as well), and Walter was an acrobat for Ringling Brothers for that one year.

Their father, Gottlieb Gollmar, was born in Germany and emigrated as a young man. He first was a driver on the Erie Canal, then moved to Chicago, where he worked for the Weber Wagon Company. In Baraboo he became a builder and contractor. He married Mary Juliar in 1846.

As we know, Ringling Brothers' Circus became a railroad operation in 1890, thus their wagon show equipment became surplus. The Gollmars purchased some of this. In addition a small circus, Fisher & Aiken, collapsed in 1890 in Iowa, and tradition has it that the brothers obtained part of it. No proof of either sale has surfaced.

When the Gollmars opened for business on May 16, 1891, in Baraboo, they had twelve wagons, three carryalls, twenty-six horses, one pony, and two mules. Their menagerie consisted of just two cages, one of which held a black bear and a leopard and the other, three monkeys. It was analogous to the size of the first Ringling circus of 1884.

As with their cousins' first circus, the Gollmars opened theirs in Baraboo and went over the bluffs to Prairie du Sac and Sauk City for their initial road movement. After several stands in Wisconsin, they went into northern Illinois, and then into Iowa. During the 1891 tenting season there were at least ten other small shows in the West, plus three large ones, Ringling, Sells Bros., and Adam Forepaugh. Half a dozen small western shows had foundered in 1890, and at least four did the same in 1891, but the Gollmars were able to make a season of it, albeit a short one.

As with the Ringlings, each Gollmar brother had a specific place in the management. Jake was the advance man, Fred the general manager, Charles the bandmaster (later the manager), Ben the treasurer, and Walter the equestrian director. Walter also appeared in the ring as clown and acrobat, and in the concert in blackface. These duties were in addition to his role as ringmaster and playing drum in the band at odd moments.

We said they had twenty-six horses that first year, but with fifteen wagons they needed about forty, so they hired teams to accompany them. This was a very common practice in wagon-show days. It was not difficult to talk a farmer's son into accompanying the circus with a team, forage and meals provided along with $5 a week. The farm boys loved the travel, and their fathers appreciated the money. Unfortunately, not being contract employees, these teamsters could leave when they became disenchanted, usually by bad weather conditions, and there was some degree of turnover among them.

In the argot of the time, the Gollmars had a twenty-five-cent show. Circuses were divided by admission prices, twenty-five cents in the case of small shows and fifty cents at larger companies. In about 1885, ten-cent circuses made their appearance. We saw that George W. Hall claimed to be the first to charge ten cents, though his one-time partner Sam McFlinn made the same claim. It is possible that the ten-cent circuses had grift. Hall did; he made up for the low admission in that way. There's an old adage that says you can't sell if you don't get them into the hall.

The Sauk County Democrat described the new circus as "a neat and clean show, free from anything objectionable," and this could have described the Gollmars' operation throughout its twenty-five-year history. They ascribed to the Ringling ethic of operating honestly and having their employees always on their good behavior.

Going into the states west of Wisconsin, the Gollmars were following the same paths for the same reasons that had lured the Mabie brothers, Burr Robbins, George Hall, and the Ringlings in their wagon-borne phases. We remarked in our discussion of the Ringlings that the prairie states were flat and the villages a day's march apart, conditions that were ideal for wagon travel. This knowledge was not a secret, and the Gollmars met many other circuses on the road. The 1891 list of shows in the West (meaning Iowa, Nebraska, Kansas, Missouri, and Minnesota) included F. J. Taylor, Wintermute Brothers, T. K. Burk, Harlburt & Leftwitch, Harris Nickel Plate, King & Franklin, and Sturtevant, Holland & Co. Most of these companies dropped by the wayside within the next few years, some in 1891.

Missouri and Iowa were much alike, "vast oceans of grasslands," as one observer called them, but in Kansas and Nebraska showmen risked dry seasons and low grass. The presence of grass was important, as the circus horses were dependent on the country for grazing. In a dry year small shows had to buy fodder, which they ordinarily did not do. The great drought of 1911, which presaged the dust bowl days of the 1930s, is the worst example of this. In three weeks in the Dakotas the Gollmars were fortunate if they made expenses. It was almost impossible to obtain hay, and what they could buy "could scarcely be handled on a fork," according to the *Grant County Herald* (Lancaster, Wisconsin). Wisconsin was not affected by the drought, and many shows fled the West to find better crop conditions.

Though the Ringling circus had the first mechanical stake driver in 1904, the Gollmars made an improvement in the basic design that was used on all subsequent machines. With the exception of the gasoline engine powering it, the Gollmars probably made the entire driver in their own quarters, such was their self-reliance and skill. Photograph, Show World, *September 21, 1907.*

The Gollmar Brothers

In their ads for the closing date in Baraboo on September 30, 1891, the Gollmars said that the season had been "one of entire satisfaction ... a year's success both in reputation and finance."

The brothers built several new wagons for 1892—literally built them, as they had Ben and Fred's carpenter experience from the furniture business to aid them. Ben was a gifted carver, and it was his work that adorned the two new bandwagons. Walter did the gilding. They went on the road with seven staff members and thirteen bill posters. There was a fourteen-piece band and an eight-piece band. Twenty-six performers traveled with them, only two of whom were well-known—Joe Parson, four-horse rider, and his wife, Clarinda Lowanda Parson, lady principal rider. Their stock was increased from the first season by fifty-five horses.

Each year saw increases in equipment, especially parade wagons, the parade being their weakest point in 1891. Since all circuses paraded, the street display was one of the aspects by which villagers judged the worth of a show. It was not unusual for the decision as to whether to buy a ticket to depend on how good the parade was thought to be. Further, people might go to the circus grounds and, after appraising the outlay, decide it wasn't worth the price of admission. An acquaintance of the authors told us that in the early years of this century, his father made a habit of looking over the circuses while they were still on the railcars, and would then decide whether or not to attend the show.

Charles Gollmar became the manager in 1893, replacing Fred, who then took over the advance. Ernest Landers, a longtime employee of the circus, described Charles Gollmar as ruling with an iron hand: "What he said went, and went big, too."

In 1893 the brothers still used the old system of having seats on one side of the ring and cages on the other. Since they had but four cages, they were not yet at the point where a separate menagerie tent was necessary. Nevertheless, a reporter suggested they put the cages elsewhere and put up more seats. Another wrote that "the menagerie part of the aggregation was a good deal of a disappointment to those people who had been gazing for two weeks or more on the flaming bill-board pictures of lions, tigers, wild-cats and other ferocious beasts." In 1895 they acquired their first elephant, named Palm. She was purchased from George W. Hall.

Almost every newspaper review of the Gollmar circus remarked on the fact of the good behavior of the employees, the absence of "skin games," "no cut-throat attachees," "a lack of characteristic toughs which are generally connected with a circus."

The comparatively small size of the early Gollmar shows, as reflected in the twenty-five-cent admission charge, also drew comments such as "best entertainment for the money," "while not the biggest one on the road it is one of the best," and "as good as can be expected for a 25 cent show." A sort of faint praise, as if the reporters hoped a big circus would soon come by. It is obvious from the encomiums in the small-town newspapers that a clean show, such as the Ringlings' or the Gollmars', was almost as good in the writers' minds as was a good performance. The majority of small circuses operated in a moral vacuum. They were not always the beneficiaries of viewers' accolades. In 1906 one wrote, "Side show was not good, but the circus and menagerie were fine." Another, in 1909, said, "The clowns were poor, and the menagerie not as good as usual." Fortunately for the company, these things were printed after the show had moved on. Over all, the Gollmars enjoyed a good press.

The circus itself had opinions about the towns and villages, though they were expressed only privately. Robert Gollmar published his uncle Ben's comments on the places they visited, and they were often uncomplimentary. A sampling from 1905 illustrates his notes:

Adrian, Michigan—rotten show town.

Clinton, Iowa—rotten show town, about 2,000 rubbernecks on lot.

Olivia, Minnesota—a Bohemian town and no good as a show town.

Long Prairie, Minnesota—Bum show town.

Tarkio, Missouri—a lot of sneak thieves and robbers here.

Balancing these places were the ones where business was good—Langdon, North Dakota; Stanley, Wisconsin; and Mondovi, Wisconsin, to name a few. If a town was a good one, the circus would visit it again. And there were usually reasons that the income was less than gratifying in some places: a train wreck in Kempton, Indiana; hard rain in Elroy, Wisconsin; haying time in Preston, Minnesota; no crops in three years in Sheldon, Iowa. Opposition from larger shows—Carl Hagenbeck, Barnum & Bailey, Gentry Brothers—was often blamed for poor receipts.

Jacob Gollmar died on the road in 1896, while serving with the advance. He left three sons—Clyde, who took over the bill posting for the rest of the year; Willis, a rider with the show; and Bert, a ticket taker. The four remaining Gollmars absorbed Jake's portion of the ownership by paying his personal debts.

As late as 1900, the Gollmars were still not much larger than when they had begun operations in 1891. Frank Macart, whom we introduced in the chapter on "Popcorn George" Hall, was in charge of the sideshow, which had but four acts, two of them by Macart and his wife, Jessie Hall Macart. There were twelve performers in the arena, presenting twenty acts with much doubling. Otto Weaver, as an example, performed on the slack rope, as a juggler, and on the flying trapeze. A second elephant had been added, named Dutch.

After ten years on the road, the circus was still confining its tours to Wisconsin, Illinois, Minnesota, Iowa, and Nebraska. Not until they went on the railroad, in 1903, did they expand the territory. They were a known quantity out in the grasslands, and they prospered from it, not reporting a bad year until 1904.

In 1901 and 1902 the title was changed to read Gollmar Bros. and Schuman's Two Big Shows. Who Schuman might have been is a mystery. There is a reference to the purchase in 1900 of Marshall Bros.' Combined Shows, and this could have been the added menagerie that Schuman supposedly contributed, yet there is no mention of a man so-named in any Gollmar roster. In preseason publicity Schuman is referred to as "the original German showman." There was a famous Schumann circus in Europe but no evidence that it ever sent animals to America. It appears to the writers that there never was a Schuman with Gollmar—no employee of the time ever referred to him—and it may be a bar sinister on the Gollmar shield.

The Gollmar Brothers

Nothing sparked the imagination on "Circus Day" like the arrival of the long string of flashy painted cars bearing the wagons of the circus. The Gollmar railroad circus, like all others originating in Wisconsin, utilized wood cars, like these sixty-footers, which are carrying the show's baggage wagons. Photograph, July 22, 1910, Hartford, Wisconsin, Circus World Museum.

The transformation to a railroad circus took place in 1903. The brothers leased fifteen railroad cars from the Ringlings, paying $260 a month. They carried 200 horses, 12 cages, 2 elephants, and 3 camels. The arena had two rings and a stage, which was the order throughout the rest of the show's existence. Old Pete, a hippopotamus leased from the Ringling brothers, died just before the 1903 season tour. Fred Gollmar located a replacement in New Jersey that belonged to the Hagenbeck animal importers and bought it, sight unseen, for $4,000. Her name was Lotus, and she trouped with the Gollmars for the next thirteen years, and with the Al G. Barnes circus for some years after that.

Because the Gollmars fed their people well and never missed a payday, their employees were very loyal, according to Robert Gollmar. The same acts returned year after year. Only the lure of higher salaries from larger firms coaxed them away. Elbridge Hocum, a horse trainer and bareback rider, joined the show in 1894; married Jake Gollmar's daughter, Maude, in 1896; and rode for the Gollmars as late as 1901. Various members of the Rooney family, Baraboo's most famous riding group, worked for the show. John Rooney was on the roster from 1900 to 1902, Charles and Frank Rooney were with it in 1905, and Charles stayed through 1909. Jenny Rooney joined in 1907, Albert Rooney in 1909. It seems that if you were a Rooney, you were a rider, and you started your career with the Gollmars.

Not just athletes were drawn to the tents. A Gollmar attaché once said, "In almost every town the management is besieged by men and boys who want to go along, and many of them offer their services for their board. It's a queer state of affairs. There is a charm, a fascination about circus life that is hard to explain. It is surely a tough existence, being buffeted about from place to place, often without a bed to sleep in, and the wages … are amazingly small. There must be a germ, bred of sawdust, that gets into the blood."

Fred Tryon, a press agent, pointed out in a 1910 article in the *Billboard* that the north and northwest territory (as it was known then) that the Gollmars visited each year was the wheat belt—Minnesota, the Dakotas, Colorado, Kansas—and at harvesttime circuses were hard put to keep their help as the wheat farmers paid much better than the showmen. However, the Gollmar brothers had no problem with this, as they treated their employees honestly.

Walter Gollmar was the most athletic of the brothers, and he performed in the ring and the concert for many years. As a young man he had joined the *Turnverein*, the imported German athletic society, one of the models for the later YMCA, and became well enough versed in acrobatics to be hired by Ringling Brothers in 1890. It was his enthusiasm that helped start his brothers in the business in 1891. As we said, he served as equestrian director, but he also performed in a triple bar act and as a clown and blackface singer. By 1893 Walter was presenting an equestrian act. His other duties, and the show's prosperity, allowed him to confine himself to the role of assistant manager by 1900.

Exotic animals like camels and elephants were carried in special circus stock cars that provided appropriate ventilation and housing for the beasts. Ring horses were moved in special "palace" cars that were fitted with partitions and feeding arrangements to ensure maximum comfort for their occupants. Photograph, July 31, 1911, Shawano, Wisconsin, Circus World Museum.

The financial panic of 1903 led to poor business in 1904 and 1905. Many small shows went under in those years. The Gollmars were disappointed enough to write to William P. Hall, the famous show buyer of Lancaster, Missouri, in 1906 that "we have no price on our show, but would like to sell next fall, if we could get what it's worth." Hall responded by asking for a price, and in October 1907 the Gollmars wrote that they hadn't made up their minds to sell. Obviously, they decided not to, as they continued in business another nine seasons. It could be that those two or three bad years had depressed the value of circus property below what the brothers expected to get for their chattels.

In a 1929 newspaper interview, Walter Gollmar said, "Transportation was probably one of the greatest difficulties with which we had to contend." He was thinking of mud, and road-less spaces, and floods, all part of trouping through the middle states. Even after switching to railroad travel, the circus had to contend with the poor condition of the western railroads. The roadbeds were unstable and the bridges of indifferent quality on many short-line roads. Circus trains, shoved in between regularly scheduled ones, were sometimes the victim of wrecks brought about because of poor communication. Since they spent most of their years in the "tor-nado belt," they suffered from windstorms from time to time. All of this was considered part of the showman's lot.

The Ringling brothers put their Adam Forepaugh & Sells Bros.' Circus in mothballs after the 1907 season. Two of their attractions they then leased to the Gollmars. One of these was the "elephant quadrille," an eight-animal troupe that had been trained by Adam Forepaugh Jr. to perform as square dancers. This addition raised the Gollmar herd to eleven elephants. The other feature was a "Fighting the Flames" show, which had a burning house and horse-drawn fire engines that rushed into the big top and doused the fire.

The show continued to be presented in two rings and a stage. By 1910 they had twen-ty-four cars in their train; they went to twenty-five in 1913. The daily expense was now $1,200 to $1,600. There were 400 employees in 1913.

Railroad travel allowed the troupe to cover three times the daily movement of a wagon show. Twenty to twenty-five miles a day was lengthened to seventy-five. They visited Montana, Oklahoma, and Colorado, places they couldn't reach with horses and wagons if they wanted to be back in Baraboo by winter.

By 1916 the twenty-five-car Gollmar circus was second only to the Ringlings' in size among Wisconsin shows, and among the ten largest in the country. Their payroll had over 400 names. Because of the World War it became difficult to maintain these figures. Experienced help was hard to find and keep. The brothers could stand up to tornadoes, floods, and train wrecks but had to give way to the exigencies of history. On the last day of the 1916 season, Gollmar Bros. Greatest of American Shows was sold in Frederickton, Missouri, to James Patterson, a Kansas carnival owner. After twenty-five years of operation, the valuable old show name was placed in the hands of others.

A MULTITUDE OF SHOWS

Following the Civil War, Wisconsin showmen came out of the woods in some numbers. Several of them, such as the Skerbeck family, literally came out of the woods because the settled area of the state had moved northward. As the great forests were cleared, logging camps and lumber mill sites became villages, serving the farms around them. The two-thirds of the state that had been forest was now the target of settlement. These late settlers coming to thin-soiled ex-timberland were mostly from eastern and southern Europe. The railroads that had been built to haul the hardwood lumber (the pine had been floated down rivers in the previous generation) to Milwaukee and Chicago now carried settlers north.

The years between the Civil War and World War I saw many circuses spring up in Wisconsin, most to fall by the wayside after a season or two. In chronicling these companies we have sometimes found fairly complete documentation, whereas for others we might have as little as one or two advertisements from newspapers. Any circus that was organized in Wisconsin qualified for this chapter, a circus being defined as a presentation in a ring of horses, acrobats, and kindred acts. Circuses are arranged here in order of their earliest appearance, and the sections are headed by the names of the proprietors.

Legions of Americans, young and old, ran away with the circus. Many more tried their hand at various circus skills, like this young man in the Iola, Wisconsin, area before the turn of the century. Photograph, undated, Iola Historical Society, Iola, Wisconsin.

This scene, showing the Holloway Bros. outfit erected on recently cleared timberland adjacent to a railroad line, was often repeated in the north woods of Wisconsin and the Upper Peninsula. As soon as outposts of civilization were accessible, the circus was soon to follow. Card photograph, 1898, Republic, Michigan, Ben Kubly Gift, Circus World Museum.

It was only by accident that Andrew Haight entered the traveling show business. By the end of his career, he had worked for several leading circuses including Adam Forepaugh, Barnum & London, and W. C. Coup. Engraving, New York Clipper, December 23, 1882.

ANDREW HAIGHT and GEORGE DeHAVEN (1865)

But for Andrew Haight (1831–1886) being a resident of Beaver Dam, where this circus was framed, the troupe was a Wisconsin show only for a matter of four weeks. It then left the state, never to return. Haight owned the Clark House hotel in Beaver Dam; DeHaven (1837–1902) was a man who talked many businessmen into financing circuses over the years. DeHaven often managed these partnerships. The Great United Circus was the sixth of such arrangements he had promoted, and as with most of them, it lasted but a single season. Haight purchased DeHaven's interest in October in New Orleans and succeeded in keeping the circus operating for another three years under the title of Haight & Chambers. Haight (nicknamed "Slippery Elm" by his contemporaries) then returned to the hotel business, but in Memphis rather than in Wisconsin. In later years he again partook of circus partnerships.

HERMAN A. FISTLER (1867–1868)

In the *New York Clipper* of October 5, 1867, there is an announcement that this company will winter on Shiel's farm, Milwaukee, Wisconsin, and start out next season with new equipment. It is the only circus reference to Fistler thus far discovered. He was at one time with the Varieties Theatre in Milwaukee.

GREENLEAF W. COLLINS (1876)

Collins (1836–1904) was a Delavan hotel proprietor who, like so many of his fellow townsmen, decided to go into the field show business. He had a small wagon show that seems not to have stirred the public. It operated but the one season.

DR. GEORGE MORRISON (1879)

Dr. Morrison (1837–1886), of Delavan, a dentist with a yen to own a circus, framed a little wagon show that not only had arenic acts, but featured the doctor doing tooth extractions and selling mouthwash. Nothing like it was ever on tour. It was managed by P. A. Older (one-time Mabie partner) and featured George Madden's magic act. The most important members of the troupe, historically, were Al Ringling, juggler, and John

Andrew Haight was one of several businessmen who was induced by showman George W. DeHaven to "angel" a circus with their cash resources. The DeHaven show ads did not acknowledge Haight's involvement. Newspaper ad, 1865, Durham Western Heritage Museum, Omaha, Nebraska.

Ringling, clown. It opened in Burlington, Wisconsin, on May 21 and folded in Green Bay in early July. Undismayed, Morrison framed a three-car railroad show that opened in Lanark, Illinois, on August 18 and closed in mid-September.

JOE PARSON and FRANK ROY (1881 and 1883)

Another small company that is more famous for its connection to the Ringlings than for anything intrinsic, this was formed by Joe Parson (1855–1895) and Frank L. Roy (1851–1936) in Darlington, Wisconsin. The organization was an outgrowth of Parson Brothers' Menagerie and Museum, which had been on tour in 1879. The Parson brothers, in addition to Joe, were Albert (1861–1933), Frank (1868–1942), George (1871–1945), and Arthur Parson (1874–1955). Al Ringling was a performer for the show in 1881, and there is some evidence that he managed it. The circus collapsed at Lake Mills, Wisconsin, in 1881. Frank Roy apparently owned the equipment, and in 1882 he placed it on the William H. Stowe circus, where it was lost in the fire that consumed the steamboat *Golden City* at Memphis on March 30, 1882. The following season Parson produced what he called "The Great Grecian Show." The circus had other titles as well. Joe Parson, a rider, did a principal riding act on Ringling Brothers from 1887 to 1889, as well as the outside free ropewalking act. His brothers were concessionaires with the Ringlings and the Gollmars for many years.

Joe Parson was a skilled rider and ropewalker who cut a dashing figure in his elegant wardrobe. The Parson shows were generally not successful, but family members made many thousands of dollars handling the concessions with two other Wisconsin circuses. Card photograph, undated, Parson Family Gift, Circus World Museum.

The smaller one-ring circuses would have looked like Dr. Morrison's Coliseum on the lot, with a single pole big top. The street procession would have focused on a single bandwagon, like this slightly decorated express wagon that had two mirrors and trim molding. Courier, 1879, Gordon Yadon Gift, Circus World Museum.

THE SKERBECK FAMILY (1884–1911)

Hurley, Iron Belt, Glidden, Park Falls, and Rib Lake were but specks on the nineteenth-century maps of Wisconsin, and so they are today. They were the typical show towns for Skerbeck's one-ring circus, which began visiting such venues in 1884. For twenty-seven years, first in wagons, later in as many as four railroad cars, this family group entertained the public in lumber, iron, and farm towns in Wisconsin, Minnesota, and Michigan's Upper Peninsula.

The family lived in Dorchester, Taylor County, Wisconsin, on land purchased sight unseen from the Wisconsin Central Railroad in 1880. Frank Skerbeck Jr. (1847–1921) and his family emigrated in 1881 and three years later launched the show that they had planned when they were still in Bohemia. Frank Skerbeck Sr. had owned a circus in Europe, and Frank Jr. had performed in it as a trapeze performer and sword swallower. He trained his children—there were sixteen of them, nine of whom lived to adulthood. All of them were performers.

Prior to the formation of the circus, the family toured hall shows in the winters, going as far as Milwaukee, Chicago, and Minneapolis, perfecting their specialties and learning to perform before the public. Antoinette, Joseph (1874–1954), and Gustav were the first of the family to appear with their father in the winter activities, and as each child approached six years of age or so, they were included, though Clara was listed as performing at three-and-a-half. Antoinette was a contortionist, Joseph was a bareback rider, and the others (Gus and Antone) were mainly acrobats.

Members of the Skerbeck troupe included (left to right) Antone, Gustav, Frank Jr., Joe, Antoinette, and Clara (front). Their ground acrobatics and other skills formed the largest part of the circus program. Photograph, 1888, Circus World Museum.

In 1884 the Skerbecks set out for their first tented season, which saw them traveling along the Wisconsin River as well as in Upper Michigan. In 1885 the family joined the Ferguson & Williams Circus of Appleton, which foundered at Sioux City, Iowa, in June of that year. With money borrowed from relatives in Europe, Frank Skerbeck launched his own show that July. Starting from Medford, Wisconsin, with ten wagons and a twelve-piece band, they were on the road until September.

The northwest reaches saw the Skerbecks in 1886 and 1888, and probably in 1887, though no information on that season has been found. They were on Eph Williams's show in 1889; in fact, the Skerbecks and Eph Williams's trained horses were most of the entertainment.

Joe Skerbeck gave an interview in which he outlined his duties on the 1889 Williams show. He gave a free act on the grounds before the doors were opened in which he walked a wire from the ground to the top of the main tent. In the performance he did a slack wire act and the single trapeze, appeared as a tumbler, and was part of several clown acts. This was not an unusual lot for a performer in such a small circus. We noted previously the number of times Walter Gollmar, for example, appeared in each performance of the Gollmar company.

Though he never did it, Frank could have limited his programs to just himself and his children. In 1900 the roster listed Frank Skerbeck, owner; Joe Skerbeck, manager; Mary

Skerbeck (1849–1931), Frank's wife, treasurer; Gus and Alice Skerbeck; Anton Skerbeck; Frank Skerbeck III; Pearl Skerbeck; Amanda Skerbeck; Clara Skerbeck—ten Skerbecks. There were twelve other performers plus a band.

Eph Williams, who was the Williams of Ferguson & Williams mentioned earlier and one of the few African-American circus proprietors in American history, had a circus in 1890 and 1891. It was titled Prof. Williams & Co.'s Consolidated German and American Railroad Shows in 1891. The Skerbecks were part of this ensemble. It traveled on three cars, a forty-foot sleeper, a flatcar, and a stock car. Their route went north into the iron country.

The next season, 1892, the Skerbecks again had their own show. It consisted of ten Skerbecks and just two other people. This was the last season of the good times that had started in 1886. The Panic of 1893 devastated the amusement business with the exception of the World's Columbian Exhibition in Chicago. Eph Williams again went on the road, and again the Skerbecks were with him, but by August the company had gone under. The family put out their own circus in August, but business was so bad they closed up and went to Chicago to play the fair.

Ed F. Davis framed a circus in New Orleans in February 1894 and hired the Skerbecks. It was the family's first appearance in the South. They made a tour of Texas, to poor business, and the Skerbecks left. (Ed F. Davis we met when he sold out to George W. Hall later in 1894. It was Davis's former elephant that attacked and crippled Hall in Cincinnati that year.) The Skerbecks transferred to a circus being conducted by Phil Diefenbach but defected when they didn't receive their promised salaries. The Panic of 1893 was still having its effect. After a short stay with a troupe operated by one "Windy" Smith, Frank Skerbeck bought and operated an Uncle Tom's Cabin company. There were many of these (called UTCs in the trade), and they were tented dramatic presentations of Harriet Beecher Stowe's novel. This was another short adventure, and Frank went back to having a circus for a few months in 1894.

Eighteen-ninety-six found the Skerbecks with Kirkhart & Rhine, a circus from Des Moines, Iowa. The season was spent on a steamer on lakes Michigan and

Though not common, major circuses occasionally bought the entire front page of a newspaper for their advertisement. Note the characteristics of the Skerbeck circus that they thought were important. Newspaper advertisement, Wausau Daily Record, 1897, *Circus World Museum.*

A diving dog and a ropewalker were the two free acts that attracted patrons to the Skerbeck circus. This may have been the railroad show the family fielded shortly after the turn of the century. Photograph, undated, Gladstone, Michigan, Circus World Museum.

Huron, mostly making stands in small Michigan towns. When they reached Detroit, the Skerbecks again formed their own show, intent on playing towns in the interior of Michigan and Wisconsin.

Frank Skerbeck then turned the company over to son Joe, who operated the Great Skerbeck Circus from 1897 to 1911, and a wild west show after that. In 1900 to 1902 the aggregation turned to railroading— Skerbeck's Great One Ring Railroad Show—but they still played in the outback of Minnesota, in Hibbing, Grand Rapids, Cass Lake, and the like, and in Wisconsin as well. Frank W. Burns had been a horse and pony trainer for the Skerbecks who organized his own circus in 1900 and hired the Skerbeck family in 1905. Burns wrote the New York Clipper, "Our route is through the iron and copper country, where we are no strangers." That was true, but he also said, "This is the first tent show to visit Northern Wisconsin and Michigan," which any Skerbeck could have told him was a false statement.

In 1907 Joe Skerbeck decided to switch from circus to wild west show, a very popular type of entertainment at that time. With the real west of Indians and cattle drives fast disappearing, American audiences were conscious that a great epoch in their history, the frontier, would soon be gone. Buffalo Bill Cody had first struck this vein of nostalgia with his Wild West in 1883. Stunningly successful as a spectacle, Cody's show gave birth to many imitators, Joe Skerbeck among them. Unfortunately, the weather would not enhance the fortunes of this new exhibition, as it proceeded to provide seven weeks of rain. At season's end the show was sold.

The family attached itself to several carnivals in 1908, hoping to replenish the exchequer so that they could afford another circus. Still working on salary, they joined a 1909 circus run by one "Oregon Red." After that, Joe, calling himself "Prairie Joe," put out Prairie Joe's Wild West Hippodrome and Circus for two seasons. They closed early in 1911, to avoid bankruptcy, again bedeviled by rain. As an example, it rained every day in northern Wisconsin from May 12 to May 25.

The family then entered the carnival business by 1915, and some members are still following that pursuit today.

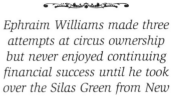

Ephraim Williams made three attempts at circus ownership but never enjoyed continuing financial success until he took over the Silas Green from New Orleans minstrel show. He retired from it in comfortable wealth and was recognized as a successful black showman in his obituary in Billboard. Courier, undated, courtesy Fred D. Pfening III.

EPH WILLIAMS (1888–1902)

A bartender and barber in the Plankinton Hotel in Milwaukee in the 1880s, Ephraim Williams (1860–1921) took up horse training as a hobby. He added ponies and dogs to his act, and at some point he decided to become a professional. His first circus, in 1888, was called Ferguson & Williams' Big Double United Monster Show. As was often the case in the nineteenth century, the longer the title, the smaller the show. Williams's partner, Ferguson, is unknown to us; the winter quarters was at Appleton, Wisconsin. They claimed thirty horses and a dozen wagons. The firm was short-lived, dissolving at Dubuque, Iowa, on July 6. It was then that Williams and the Skerbeck family, using the former dressing tent as a big top, played Iowa, as we mentioned earlier. The chattels of the Ferguson–Williams show were bought by R. Z. Orton.

Williams & Co. was the title of the 1889 effort, another Appleton-based circus. It traveled on two railroad cars, and most of the cast was made up of Skerbecks. At season's end the company went into Medford, Wisconsin, which was Williams's winter quarters for some years. His 1890 show was mounted on three cars, had the Skerbecks once more, and traveled through the iron country, across northern Wisconsin and into the Dakotas. Frank Skerbeck became the show treasurer in 1891, indicating that he owned part of the show. Eight Skerbecks were in the lineup.

The largest of the circuses that Eph Williams had was his 1892 and 1893 Prof. Williams' Consolidated Railroad Shows. On five cars, with a fifteen-cage menagerie and fifteen performers, the 1892 show left Medford on May 5. Oddly enough, there are no reports from this ensemble in the trade papers of that year. After a year away from Williams, the Skerbecks returned to his fold in 1893. This time there were twelve of them. It was a bad year in the amusement business, just as it was on Wall Street, and Williams gave up the endeavor in July.

There is an announcement in the Medford paper in 1896 that Williams was taking over the bar in the Hotel Winchester, so he was out of the field show business in that year. We don't find him again until 1897, and that through a newspaper ad in Medford. Williams

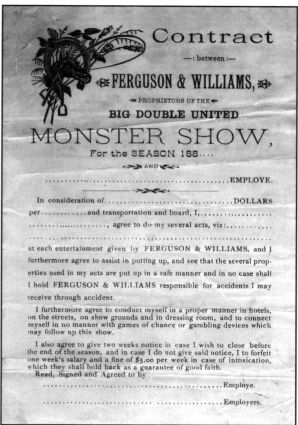

Many different contracts were printed for circus use, including forms for feed, lodging, lot rental, and so on. This very rare and simple employee contract form is one of the few surviving paper remnants of the first black-owned circus to be framed in the U.S. It included both work scope and conduct considerations. Contract form, 1888, Circus World Museum.

attached himself, and his horses and ponies, to the Skerbeck One Ring Show in 1900 but was back with his own troupe in 1901. Williams & Co.'s Great Northern Show was on five cars and was framed in Milwaukee instead of Medford. Williams had married in 1892, and his wife was a schoolteacher in Milwaukee, where their children were raised, and he may have decided to move his headquarters. The show was out again in 1902. That proved to be Eph Williams's last circus.

He turned to a tented minstrel show—Silas Green from New Orleans—with which he made the proverbial fortune. He died a wealthy man in Florida. Famous as the first African American to have a successful circus career, he was well-known in the business for once having bested "Popcorn George" Hall in a business deal. Apparently no one else had ever done it.

HARRY CASTELLO (1889–1915)

Harry G. Castello (1866?–1920) may have been a son of the famous Dan Castello of Racine. On occasion he was referred to as Dan Castello Jr. At any rate, he was Mrs. Dan Castello's son. Ben Hecht, the famous playwright and journalist, lived in Mrs. Castello's house in Racine when he was a child, and his memories of Harry Castello are an interesting read.

> He was my first mentor, and I write his name with tenderness. Harry was a trapeze performer. He lay all winter in his bed in an overheated little back room, reading "nickel novels" and drinking beer. In the spring he rose from his bed and started getting in condition again. Harry was the first to stir ambition in me. He aroused in me the desire to be an acrobat. For three years, until I was fourteen, Harry instructed me in a routine as a "single." The trapeze hung in the barn behind the house.

> In the summer of my fourteenth year, Harry and a troupe of acrobatic jacks-of-all-trades got together enough money to take a one-ring tent show on the road. I went as part of the troupe.

> I did my soloing on the trapeze for the next two months until bankruptcy overtook our circus. On the way to Fond du Lac it mysteriously disintegrated—its tent, its blue-painted rows of flap-down seats, its thousands of feet of heavy ropes and various pieces of unsatisfactory equipment, all disappearing along with my genial and arthritic colleagues of the sawdust.

That was 1908, but years before that Harry Castello was on the road with the P. T. Barnum show as a boy rider. Of course, Dan Castello was a partner of Barnum's and in charge of the circus portion of that huge aggregation. This was in 1871 and 1872. In 1884 Harry was a featured performer on G. W. Hall's Consolidated Shows, presenting a ceiling-walking act. Under the name Castello & Co. of Racine, Harry advertised for performers for a projected minstrel show in 1888.

The *New York Clipper* called him Dan Castello Jr. in 1889 and said he had a wagon show on tour. There are advertisements for Marion & Castello's Interocean in 1896. He is found in 1898 on Marshall Bros.' Shows, again doing a ceiling walk.

The stretches of time between any news of Castello may mean he was off the road (reading nickel novels) or spending his time with small shows of which no notice reached the trade papers.

Castello & Co.'s R.R. Shows went out of Racine in 1907, and the unnamed group that Hecht was with is dated 1908. And there was another such circus in 1909. Harry's 1915 effort, Castello's Great Western Show, foundered because of bad weather and under-capitalization. "The elements were against me," he was quoted as saying in a Baraboo paper. An employee made the statement to *Billboard* that Harry was drunk the whole five days of the firm's existence. What capital there was had been supplied by two Burlington saloon keepers who appeared on the lot and packed up all the equipment.

Presumably that 1915 show was Harry's last. In 1920 he shot himself, according to Ben Hecht.

GIBBONS & CHAPMAN (1889)

This circus was framed in Janesville, Wisconsin. It began the season on May 4, played at Brodhead May 7, and collapsed at Mineral Point on May 13. *Sic transit Gloria.*

It was unusual for a circus as small as McDonald's to play a community as large as Milwaukee. Typically they would exhibit on a number of different show grounds within the community, playing the various neighborhoods. Their advertisements reflected the relative size of the circus. Newspaper advertisement, 1889, Circus World Museum.

CHARLES C. McDONALD (1889)

Claiming to be "the largest, most complete, massive, entertaining, diversified, classic, original, novel, and pleasing circus now traveling the West," this one-ring show was organized in Milwaukee. Charles C. McDonald was the managing partner; his wife did a principal act of horsemanship. Two investors in the firm were Jacob Litt (1849–1905), operator of a Milwaukee dime museum, and his press agent, Will A. Innes (d. 1889) of Grand Rapids, Michigan. Their opening on June 1 was greeted with several days of rain, despite which they reported good business. As in Chicago, it was possible to play several lots in Milwaukee in various neighborhoods, which they did. After Milwaukee, the show "toured the North," including Escanaba, Michigan, and returned after several weeks to Milwaukee. Then they visited Racine and Rockford, Illinois, and were last reported in Chicago in September. A December note in the *New York Clipper* verified that the circus had failed.

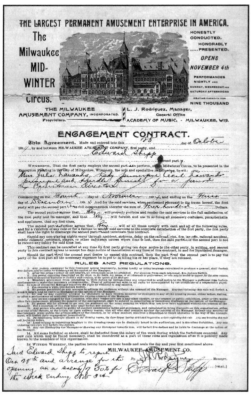

One of Milwaukee's two resident indoor circuses was L. J. Rodriguez's 1894 effort. He hired experienced winter circus proprietor Edward Shipp of Petersburg, Illinois, to assist him in managing the circus. It lasted but a short time, but there was no lack of attention to employee rules of behavior. Engagement contract, 1894, Edward Shipp Papers, Dorothy Douglass Gift, Circus World Museum.

THE MILLER BROTHERS (1889–1891)

In his memoirs, published in 1928, a performer named W. Q. Hendricks tells a story of accepting a contract to perform for the Millers in 1889. It is the only proof there is of the existence of the circus in that year. The Miller brothers, of Beaver Dam, Wisconsin, were Alfred (1856–1930), Charles (1854–1919), and Otto (1862?–1934). Charles C. Miller was a lawyer who owned a bookstore and musical instrument business in Beaver Dam. The other two at one time billed themselves as "Al and Otto, the Funny Clowns," which seems to be a redundancy. The earliest notice of them in the trade press is dated 1891. In that year they called their aggregation Miller Bros.' American and German Allied Shows. Theirs was a wagon show, intended to tour Wisconsin, Iowa, and Nebraska. One account has them closing forever at Bushy Creek, Iowa, in 1892. Charles Miller operated a theatre in Beaver Dam for twenty-five years. Al (Alf) Miller remained in the circus business for some years.

L. J. RODICUE/RODRIGUEZ (1889 and 1894)

Calling himself "the Barnum of all small shows," Rodicue advertised for performers in the *New York Clipper* on May 11, 1889, expecting to open in Milwaukee on June 3. In fact, he began the season on June 9 and by July 23 was stranded at Green Bay. The circus was abandoned on the lot, and much of the property was stolen. The man who had lent the equipment sued in the amount of $1,000. Rodicue was an assumed name of Lawrence J. Rodriguez, theatre man from Milwaukee. He and four other men, including the one-time (actual-

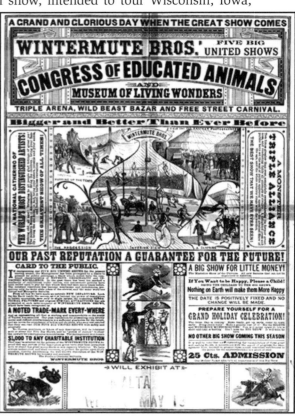

Wonderful in its excess of detail, the mere layout of the circus couriers of the nineteenth century excited readers. Circus bill creators utilized an abundance of different fonts more than a century before the first word processors made a multitude of choices possible. Courier, 1892, Earl Chapin May Gift, Circus World Museum.

ly, five-time) mayor of Milwaukee, David S. Rose, formed a corporation that operated what they called The Midwinter Circus in 1894. They leased the Exposition Music Hall for a cold-weather show at $1,000 a month. A tent was erected in the hall and bleacher seats provided for the audience. The best-known participant was George Holland's riding act. Opening night was a sellout, but subsequent audiences were described as "only fair." The circus closed January 6, 1895, after eight weeks.

The wagon-based advertising crew of the Wintermute-owned Great Melbourn show is proudly displaying the special multiple sheet portrait bill of the show owners. Each day they would set out on their country routes erecting magnificent stands of vibrantly colored circus lithographs. Cabinet photograph, 1904, Zella Wintermute Hall Gift, Circus World Museum.

THE WINTERMUTE BROTHERS (1889–1913)

First organized in Whitewater, Wisconsin, this was a partnership among Halsey (1867–1961), Harry (1861–1939), and Thomas (1862–1905) Wintermute. It began as a hall show carried on one wagon and grew into a seventeen-wagon circus by 1902. Halsey was the advance man, Harry was a magician and ventriloquist, and Thomas was an acrobat and juggler. As with so many of these small Wisconsin circuses, the Wintermutes traveled Wisconsin, Minnesota, the Dakotas, and Iowa. At the end of the 1891 season they put into Hebron, Wisconsin, for the winter, which became their headquarters. Forty horses pulled the wagons in 1890; by 1892 they were up to sixty. Ten bandsmen discoursed the music, and ten billposters assisted Halsey Wintermute. They described 1893 as their tenth annual season. If true, that means they put the hall show out for the first time in 1882.

By 1896 the Wintermute family itself was able to present seven acts, half of a normal circus program. They offered a return act on trapeze (in which the flyer leaves a trapeze for the grip of the catcher, then returns to the original bar), a double trapeze act (two people at different heights), a high-wire act, a slack-wire routine, a tranca act (in which the performer lies on his back and juggles a wooden cross—the tranca—with his feet), and juggling. They needed only nine other people for their full program.

In reading the rosters of a circus such as Wintermutes, one is struck by the anonymity of the personnel. Name after name appears that just as quickly disappears. Even a seasoned researcher finds none that have any future in the business. It is as if their one bright moment of fame came in their listing

Here is an example of the Wintermute billposting crew's handiwork, an outstanding "hit" for the Thursday, June 9, 1904, date at Bush City, Minnesota. Bill stands featured exciting graphics to catch the eye, along with the show's title and the day, date, and location of the engagement. Cabinet photograph, 1904, Zella Wintermute Hall Gift, Circus World Museum.

with this obscure wagon show. Reading these rosters is tantamount to reading old baseball scorecards or newspaper society news. We would not be surprised to learn that the predominant reason for many of these athletes to subscribe to the rigors of circus life was simply to escape the farms and kitchens and small towns that otherwise would be their lifelong lot. Every village had at least one hero, whether soldier, ballplayer, actor, or circus performer.

For reasons yet to be known, the Wintermutes changed the name of their circus to The Great Melbourne United Shows in 1901 (it was sometimes spelled "Melbourn"). They said their band was "small, but noisy." In 1902 they had rain for the first sixty-three days of the season. Though they had pony, dog, and goat acts throughout their history, mainly because brother Thomas was an expert at this, they hired no riders before 1915, a strange situation. Their first elephant, named Jargo, appeared in advertising in 1907; he belonged to Frank Hall, Popcorn's son. Clarence H. Black was listed as co-manager in that same year and may have bought an interest, as the *New York Clipper* called the show Wintermute & Black Great United Shows. At season's end Harry Wintermute bought out all the others and for 1908 restored the Melbourn title.

George W. Hall Jr. entered the picture in 1909, becoming co-manager with Harry Wintermute for one season. Frank Hall was the equestrian director and still had his elephant. Thomas Wintermute Jr. was in charge of the stock.

Frank E. Hall married Zella Wintermute, the sister of the family, in 1912. They established their home in Whitewater, and Frank became a partner of Harry Wintermute. Zella became the show treasurer. The title became Wintermute Bros. & Hall's Wagon Show, the winter quarters of which was now in Fort Atkinson. This was the order of things beginning in 1914. Zella not only handled the money, but presented the elephant in the ring. In 1915 the first mention of a riding act was made.

Through all the years before 1914 the show had a twenty-five-cent admission, and in that year it went to thirty-five cents. Always a one-ring circus, it traveled on fifteen wagons (plus two for the advance) from 1902 until it closed in 1917. As we said in our history of the Hall family, Frank and Zella Hall owned Vanderburg Bros.' Circus in the 1920s.

Five sets of brothers preceded the Ringlings in the circus business, but the Ringlings were the ones who made "Bros." a significant circus title component. Among the Wisconsin brothers who followed in their wake were the Stangs, who emphasized the nostalgia of the old-time one-ring circus. Letterhead, 1907, Circus World Museum.

THE STANG BROTHERS (1892 and 1897)

Al Ringling might take credit for the entry of the three Stang brothers into the circus business. In 1879 Lorenz Stang (1855–1940) joined Dr. Morrison's Coliseum (see earlier entry) as a teamster. Al took a liking to the young man and taught him how to juggle. Once he mastered this, over the following winter, Stang decided to become a professional, or so the family tradition has it. He is not in any of the usual records before 1892 but did have a sideshow on tour in 1887. In the 1892 season he and his brother Frank (1858–1923) formed Stang Brothers One-Ring Circus. With four or five wagons they departed their hometown, Burlington, Wisconsin, after opening there on May 7. By June 29 they were back home. It had rained thirty-nine of the fifty-two days they were out. In addition, their tent had been blown down in Kirkland, Illinois, on June 22.

This experience satisfied the brothers until 1897, when they tried again. This time a third brother, Valentine (1851–1916), went along. As in 1892, their wagons were built by William Peters, a Burlington blacksmith. They traveled on eighteen wagons. Business was reported as less than satisfactory in Racine, Kenosha, and Milwaukee. Once again they closed early, being back in Burlington by July 3. This time it was lack of funds that doomed the enterprise. The performers had received little of their pay since they had opened and were owed $1,200. The brothers had neglected to obtain a state license ($100 annual fee) and didn't have that much in the kitty when a treasury agent came visiting. With a state lien on the property and the refusal of the employees to work until their back pay was restored, the season abruptly ended.

Close inspection of this interior view of the Holloway big top reveals a number of performance apparatus including tumbling mats, nested trapeze bars, and an elevated ladder and rings. The Holloways, who are likely the balancing group in the center, presented most of the acts comprising the performance. Card photograph, circa 1899, Norway, Michigan, Burt Holloway Gift, Circus World Museum.

Frank and Ed Holloway were doing acrobatics with the Wintermute show the year this portrait was taken. It was common for Wisconsin circus performers to travel with fellow Badger state showmen when they lacked the necessary capital to tour their own circus. Over-painted photograph, 1896, Circus World Museum.

THE HOLLOWAY BROTHERS (1893–1897)

The five Holloway brothers, from Birnamwood, Wisconsin, were on various circuses over the decade 1893 to 1903, and in addition they had their own company from time to time. Because they didn't always work together, their history is somewhat convoluted. Art, Claude, Frank, Ed, and Max were accomplished acrobats, usually appearing as trapeze performers, but were capable of other routines, including wirewalking, riding, and presenting trained ponies and dogs, nor was clowning beyond their abilities.

They took their own circus out of Hebron, Wisconsin, in 1893 and 1894. They left it in the barn in 1895 in order to go out with George Hall, Jr.'s Trained Animal Show. The fourth brother, Ed, had been with Hall in 1894 as a contortionist.

Art, Claude, Frank, and Ed were on Wintermute Bros. Circus in 1896, with Claude acting as bandmaster in addition to his duties with his brothers. Then, in 1897, they were with Stang Bros.' One-Ring Show and Claude was again a band member. Stang Bros. went under in Hartford, Wisconsin, before the season was well under way, so the Holloways put their own circus back in action. They were out in 1898 and 1899 as well. Their title was Holloway Bros. New United Shows, Claude, manager; Ed, assistant manager; Frank, rider; and Max, trick pony and mules. They said they would tour "our old stamping grounds" in 1897, meaning Wisconsin, northern Michigan, Iowa, and Illinois.

As with most small-show proprietors, the Holloways could not sit idle in the winter; their profits were not that large. Together, or as singles, they appeared in various winter shows, some under their own management. Max Holloway, the youngest of the brothers, developed a Jackley act, with which he played winter shows. In this he dropped headfirst from a sixteen-foot ladder, landed on his hands on a table, and turned a series of handsprings to a mat on the ground. Art Holloway did a similar act.

In 1901 and 1902, Frank and Ed were on Ringling with a high-wire act labeled "The Holloways." In 1902, Claude Holloway was bandleader with Frank Hall's United Wagon Shows out of Nora Springs, Iowa. The contract survives; he was paid $10 per week.

Robert V. Hall (no relation to the Evansville Halls) had a circus in Fond du Lac in 1903 and other years, and Arthur, Claude, and Max were with him. In 1903 Frank organized the Frank Holloway Comedy Company to play halls and opera houses in the summer. In 1907, Frank and Ed were again with Ringling.

ANTHONY WHITE (1894)

In Milwaukee on May 1, 1894, "Professor Tony" White (born Anthony Whittfelder White, 1857–1930) opened a circus that traveled on twelve wagons. White had a five-horse liberty act as well as a pair of comic mules. He had previously been on the musical stage and at one time was a Punch and Judy operator. His obituary named several circuses that he had worked for, but the only one we could confirm was Skerbeck's in 1903.

THE MARSHALL BROTHERS (1896–1899)

This organization was an outgrowth of Marshall Brothers Medicine Co., which had operated in Cleveland, Ohio, but was moved to Avoca, Wisconsin, in 1893. The brothers of the title were Charles, Edward, Michael, and William Marshall, sons of Matthew Marshall. For three seasons, 1889 to 1891, they were with the Ringling Brothers'

Mike, Charley, Will, and Ed Marshall stand behind their parents, Mr. and Mrs. Matt Marshall in 1892. They were best known as bandsmen on many different circuses and wild west shows. Photograph, 1892, Matt Marshall Gift, Circus World Museum.

band, and subsequently with other circuses. Their own effort may have begun in 1896; a letter from a descendant uses that date, but no printed materials or newspaper accounts have been found dated prior to 1897. All four brothers were musicians and performed as acrobats as well. In addition, William Marshall was a contortionist. As with other small companies we've described, the owner's family performed most of the acts on the program. A circa-1897 photo shows fourteen people plus the eight-piece band. Marshall Bros. Shows was sold to the Gollmars in early 1900. The individual brothers then hired out as bandsmen to circuses throughout the country.

WILLIAM J. ASH (1897)

Framed in Racine, Wisconsin, by William J. Ash (or Ashe, 1871–1953) of Toledo, Ohio, Greatest United Shows charged only twenty cents admission (children, ten cents). Ash had made his mark in show business as the leader of the Flying Ashtons, a trapeze troupe. This 1897 effort lasted but a few weeks.

HERBERT L. MARSHALL (1897)

Housed in the Panorama Building in Milwaukee, Circus Royal opened May 22 with a run-of-the-mill roster and was not a success.

Burns, Boldt, and Hanus were men of completely different backgrounds who pooled their money and talents to launch a modest circus in 1900. Hanus later owned and operated a number of theaters in Antigo and other northern Wisconsin communities. Contract, 1900, John Hanus Gift, Circus World Museum.

F. W. BURNS (1900–1905)

In 1900 the Burns, Boldt & Hanus Famous Circus was formed in Antigo, Wisconsin, by three gentlemen with no experience in field show operation. Fred W. Burns (1864?–1943) was a pool hall operator in Wausau, Fred W. Boldt (1876–1961) was a store clerk, and John Hanus (1878–1957) was an Antigo farmer. They were inspired by a horse belonging to Burns that was so highly trained it performed almost without guidance. The little thirteen-wagon show was out twelve weeks with little profit. Burns then leased his stock to Skerbeck's One-Ring Circus in 1901 and 1902. The next season he went on tour with his own F. W. Burns & Co.'s New Railroad Show. He had this company on the road in 1904 and 1905 as well. We mentioned earlier that the Skerbeck family joined him in 1905. Burns advertised them as "the greatest acrobats in the world." By July the troupe was augmented by a menagerie and a third railroad car. This proved to be the extent of Burns's circus career. He opted for the vaudeville circuits in 1906, a venture he followed until he retired in 1915. Fred Burns died in Terre Haute, Indiana, in 1943.

ROBERT V. HALL (1902–1906)

A native of Fond du Lac, Wisconsin, where he had his winter quarters, R. V. Hall (1863–1944) was a talented musician who once advertised a concert in which he would play eight different instruments. In May 1902 he bought something called the Royal Show at Des Moines, Iowa, and changed its name to Hall's Big Tent Show, opening the season in Fond du Lac on June 9. It isn't clear what this was, hall show or circus, but its vaudeville aspect was pronounced. In 1903 he had the R. V. Hall Shows on the road, which was a circus that used two railroad cars but had no horse acts. The route was in northern Wisconsin. No notices have been found for 1904 or 1905, but the company was on the road in 1906 under the title R. V. Hall's Circus.

Show owner Robert Hall is in the white hat near the ticket window. Robert Engfer, who did a contortion act for Hall, is seated seventh from the right. He changed his name to Engford and became another Wisconsin circus owner. Cabinet photograph, 1903, Frank and Ruth Engford Clark Gift, Circus World Museum.

EMIL SEIBEL (1903–1916)

Dog and pony shows were a subgenre of the circus business that was extremely popular in the early years of the twentieth century. Based on the idea of a circus in miniature, these lilliputian productions used ponies, dogs, goats, and monkeys in place of the horses, lions, tigers, and other large animals carried by full-sized shows. Their wagons were smaller and their cages built in miniature, and if they had elephants, they were very small ones. Except for the animal trainers, dog and pony shows as a rule had no human performers, though they did carry bands. Henry B. Gentry of Bloomington, Indiana, had the most famous such troupe, Gentry's Dog and Pony Show, which he started in 1887 as a theatre act. Eventually, Gentry had as many as four such shows on the road at one time. The Gentry name was before the public over fifty years.

The diminutive wagons and a small elephant emphasized the child appeal of the Seibel Bros. dog and pony operation. A diving dog was the free act that used the ladder on the right. Photograph, undated, Zella Wintermute Hall Gift, Circus World Museum.

Children were especially enthralled by these small-scale circuses, and managers liked them because they were inexpensive to operate. Two railroad cars could carry such a show, and animal feed was inexpensive compared to what it cost to operate a menagerie. Emil Seibel (1857–1922) of Watertown, Wisconsin, operated Seibel Bros.' Dog and Pony Show for fourteen years, though late in his career he opted for full-size circuses. A merchant and landowner in Watertown, where he was born, Seibel was a fancier of ponies and built a large herd of them. Circuses were customers of his pony sales. The death of Seibel's first wife caused him to sell his store and cast about for something less stressful to occupy himself. Why he would choose operating a dog and pony show as a lessening of commercially induced stress eludes us. There were no brothers in the management; Seibel and his son, Edward (1882–1921), were the managers. Romeo Sebastian trained the animals.

In his first ad for help Seibel said he needed a clown and a blackface comedian, indicating that he was going to have a sideshow. The wagon-borne outfit, much of it purchased from one Charles Berkell of Des Moines, Iowa, started out in May 1903 with seventy-five ponies and thirty-five dogs. Twenty full-sized draft horses pulled the wagons over the road. Admission was twenty-five cents and fifteen cents. Despite a season of much rain, the Seibels pronounced their first tour a success.

The dog and pony show was offered at auction on December 3, 1903. The reason for this was seen in the new title that opened the 1904 season, Seibel Bros.' New Railroad Shows. Three times as large, the ads proclaimed, but it was still a presentation mainly of ponies, dogs, and monkeys. Edward Seibel had become the trainer and had added a horse act. As with most dog and pony shows, children in the audience were allowed to ride the ponies at the conclusion of the performance. Two seventy-foot railroad cars carried the exhibition.

The 1905 tour, a successful one, was routed into the South for the entire season. They had a short tour in 1906, said to be because of bad weather. By September they were back in quarters in Watertown. A combination with one of Henry B. Gentry's dog and pony units was arranged for 1907. This season was spent in the South and Southwestern part of the country. Emil Seibel went back to sole proprietorship in 1908.

An attempted lease of the show to two inexperienced showmen, Cooper and Robenson, in May 1909 resulted in a one-day fiasco from which Seibel had to reclaim his chattels. He may have sat out the season.

Nineteen-ten was spent in the South, the show returning to Watertown in December. Edward Seibel had, for an unknown period, operated Edwards Bros.' Animal Show in northern states and Canada, perhaps as a way to show his training ability. For 1911 Seibel Bros. and Edwards Bros. were combined in Seibel Bros.' United Shows.

We have seen all sorts of "Brothers" titles in this chronology, some actually involving fraternal partners, others, such as Seibel's, not having such relationship. It would seem that the phenomenal success of the Ringling brothers circus contributed to this usage, but it was also a commercial habit of the times to identify relationships in company titles. "And Brothers," "and Sons" were commonly seen on store signs and manufacturing letterheads. Such combinations showed solidity and purpose, it is assumed.

By 1912 Seibel Bros.' show had a more pronounced circus aspect, as they added human performers to the many dog and pony acts. There was a strongman, a contortionist, and a slack-wire performer in that season. Edward Seibel once more split his Edwards Bros.' Animal Show from his father's troupe in 1913 and followed a separate route, going again into Canada.

Seibel ended railroad travel in 1914, as well as in 1915. He reverted to wagons, using about thirty of them, and a train of about thirty ponies. The novelty of dog and pony shows was wearing thin at this time, and attendance was down from the years before. This was partly the result of the growing number of large circuses, the competition between which was causing them to play in smaller venues, thus squeezing the little troupes out of profitable areas. In 1916, Seibel Bros. was one of the last of the dog and pony shows on the road.

In March 1917 the wagons, stock, and equipment of Seibel Bros.' Greater Shows was auctioned in Watertown. Emil Seibel bought a farm near Weyauwega, Wisconsin, and his and Edward's families moved there. Edward died in August 1921, and his father followed him ten months later.

GEORGE E. WAGNER (1905–1914)

Using the stage name of "Jolly Jenaro," George Wagner (1879?–1934) made a career as a clown and comic juggler. He began about 1890 and was with the Bostock carnival in 1901 and R. V. Hall's tent show in 1903. In 1905 he organized Wagner Bros.' Old Time One Ring Shows in conjunction with his four brothers. The show was more a variety presentation than a true circus, featuring acrobats, trapezists, clowns, and songs. It was a wagon show. Wagner's wife was the treasurer, his brother Herman had the privileges, brother Albert was the contractor, and brother Luther was with the

It was typical for performers to own and operate circuses, particularly those with horse skills. George Wagner, "Jolly Jenaro," was Wisconsin's only clown to own and operate a traveling circus. Letterhead, 1902, Circus World Museum.

advance. The company wintered in Milwaukee until early 1909, when it was moved to Germantown, Ohio. They stayed in Ohio until 1912, when they moved back to Milwaukee. In that year they stopped using a ring, substituting a stage, which certainly took them out of the circus classification. However, Wagner played fair dates with a miniature circus of ponies, dogs, and monkeys each fall and winter. After 1914 the name Great Wagner Shows does not appear. Twenty years later, in August 1934, Wagner committed suicide after his wife was granted a divorce.

CARL M. DALTON (1908)

Carl Dalton was best known for his managing of traveling theater companies, particularly those which were based on nationality stereotypes. In the course of his work he was hired by John Hanus, who had just concluded his circus career. Letterhead, undated, courtesy John Hanus.

The Yankee American Show, from La Crosse, Wisconsin, was a combination of a wagon show with automobile transportation. Two touring cars carried the performers from town to town, and a large automobile bandwagon carried the musicians. In addition, the tents and other properties were carried in eighteen horse-drawn wagons. It was a two-ring aggregation that had two notable aspects. The first of these was that William Lindemann was the equestrian director (though there were no horse acts). In 1920 Lindemann Bros.' Circus (see later entry) used as a subtitle Yankee American Shows. This was Wisconsin's first truck show and may have used Carl Dalton's equipment as well as his idea of automobile transportation. Dalton (1872–1948) had previously toured a theatre company.

The second aspect of interest was that Dalton seems to have introduced the comic act, which many shows subsequently copied, called "Jargo the Giraffe." This was the presentation of two men in a giraffe costume, which can still be seen today. The "Jargo" name came to be the designation for this act.

Lindemann persevered, as we said, and "Jargo" became a circus institution, but Dalton's Yankee American Show toured Wisconsin until August 1908 and then folded its tents forever.

DODE FISK (1909–1910)

Theodore "Dode" Fisk (1859–1941) of Wonewoc, Wisconsin, came into circus ownership through a trained horse named DeCryon. He exhibited the horse at fairs and horse shows as a free grandstand show. Later, he had another trained horse, Bobbie, which he sometimes put under canvas and charged a fee for admission. This led to a dog and pony show in 1906, which was a wagon-borne outfit. After two seasons under this arrangement, Fisk enlarged his show and put it on rails. From this it was but a step to operate a circus, which he did in 1909 and 1910.

Fisk's father, Nathan, was a wealthy property owner in Wonewoc on whose Black Rock Farm Dode kept his racehorses and his tented shows. Dode was an only child and seems, in retrospect, to have been indulged in just about anything he wanted to do. He had a successful dance band on winter tour, he followed the races, and after he left the circus business he and his wife traveled about, giving lessons in ballroom dancing. The slogan he used in 1907 was as follows: "It attracts the wise, charms the ladies, delights the children, and amazes all." That description would also apply to Fisk personally, it would seem.

Henry Jr. and Corwin Moeller, first cousins to the Gollmar and Ringling brothers, constructed and repaired wagons for a number of circuses, wild west shows, and carnivals. Here are the bandwagon, racing chariots, tableaus, cage, and baggage wagons they fabricated for the Dode Fisk Show in 1909. Cabinet photograph, 1909, Baraboo, Wisconsin, Henry Moeller Gift, Circus World Museum.

The 1906 dog and pony show was larger than many of the Wisconsin circuses we have described. It had sixty-four horses, a fifteen-piece band, and seven human performers as well as all the ponies, dogs, and monkeys of an ordinary dog and pony show. In 1908 the train had seven cars and an elephant named Ding. George Chindahl has written that the firm made 163 stands that year from Wisconsin to Mississippi.

Fisk's 1909 circus was a thirteen-car, two-ring show that had a sideshow and a menagerie tent. Performers of some renown, such as Mike Rooney, the rider, and the Loretta twins, trapeze artists, were on the payroll. The 1910 Dode Fisk offering varied little from that of the previous season, but it followed a long route into the Southwest, ending up in Brenham, Texas, in December. Preparations for the 1911 season were under way when it was announced that Fisk had sold the show to Jerry Mugivan. It became Sanger Bros. Circus in 1911.

CORLISS BULGER and DUDLEY CHENEY (1911)

Corliss F. Bulger (b. 1874) and Dudley Cheney (1879–1943) were partners in what was first planned to be a dog and pony show but proved to be a full-fledged circus that existed for most of one season. Based in Sparta, Wisconsin, the new eight-car show was financed by Cheney's father, a Wisconsin banker. There were many goat, pony, and dog acts, testifying to the original intent, but there were also the standard riding, trapeze, and acrobatic performances. The show collapsed on July 6, partly a victim of the drought that

Dode Fisk looked very elegant when he presented his trained horses in the ring. One cannot imagine how he was able to keep his wardrobe in outstanding condition given the unpredictable mix of weather and circus show grounds. Cabinet photograph, undated, courtesy Wonewoc Public Library, Wonewoc, Wisconsin.

devastated Minnesota and the Dakotas. It was reorganized to open again July 26, only to close for good on September 11. The remnants became J. H. Garrett's Rice Bros. circus of 1912.

THE BEVERUNG BROTHERS (1914)

A Milwaukee circus, Beverung Brothers was owned by Robert and Irving Beverung and Harry E. Billings. They advertised that 1914 was their third year, but they must have been counting their personal careers in some way, as the circus was on the road but the one season. Their plan was to play two months on various Milwaukee lots and then make the county fair circuit. A tornado in Wauwatosa, Wisconsin, a suburb of Milwaukee, ended the season on June 30 and, as it transpired, ended the circus itself. The management said they would try again the next year, but they did not.

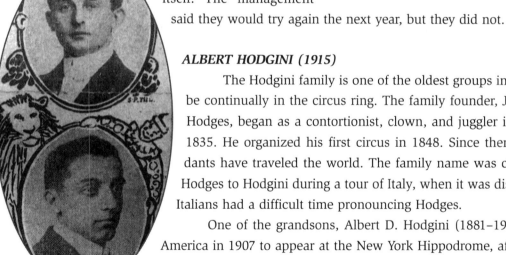

Dud Cheney's father was a banker and likely supplied most of the capital needed to frame the Bulger & Cheney operation. Their plan to build a dog and pony show expanded into a complete circus. Letterhead, 1911, William P. Hall Papers, Mrs. William Bunch Gift, Circus World Museum.

Robert (top) and Irving Beverung were involved with Milwaukee's Majestic Theatre before they made their 1914 foray into the circus business. Photograph, 1914, Circus World Museum.

ALBERT HODGINI (1915)

The Hodgini family is one of the oldest groups in the world to be continually in the circus ring. The family founder, Joseph Henry Hodges, began as a contortionist, clown, and juggler in England in 1835. He organized his first circus in 1848. Since then his descendants have traveled the world. The family name was changed from Hodges to Hodgini during a tour of Italy, when it was discovered that Italians had a difficult time pronouncing Hodges.

One of the grandsons, Albert D. Hodgini (1881–1963), came to America in 1907 to appear at the New York Hippodrome, after which he presented his riding act on the Keith vaudeville circuit. John Ringling hired Hodgini for the 1908 season and had him as an employee through 1914. Hodgini appeared six or seven times in the program; his most famous act was "The Original Miss Daisy," in which he performed a bareback act dressed as a woman. Having spent his winters in Baraboo, Albert launched his own circus from there in 1915. It was a railroad show, on two cars. The *Billboard* said of it, "A good show with a strong lineup of headline acts." Framed for the small towns, the circus spent June in Wisconsin, July in Minnesota and South

Dakota, August in Iowa and Missouri, September and October in Oklahoma, and December in Louisiana. The question as to why the circus played but the one long season has never been answered.

H. R. J. MILLER (1919–1922)

"Ben," the riding bear, was the feature of Herman Miller's one-ring wagon show in 1919, its first season. The circus went out of Wilton, Wisconsin, with fewer than ten performers (all doubling, of course), including owner Miller's trained horse. If the troupe was touring in 1920, no sign of it has been discovered, but they were at it again in 1921 using the title H. R. J. Miller's American Circus and featuring a sixteen-piece band. In 1922 Miller (d. 1957) used eight wagons and lighted his tents with electricity for the first time. This was also the last time, as the circus did not tour again.

The two-car Hodgini Shows performance included Baraboo residents such as the Rooney aerial act and the Hodginis themselves. They opened by playing the lots in Chicago suburbs. Herald, 1915, Barry Dubuque Gift, Circus World Museum.

Herman Miller probably trained most of the animal acts for his own circus. The light wagons of his hybrid overland and motorized operation serve as a backdrop. Letterhead, 1921, Circus World Museum.

THE ENGFORD FAMILY (1920–1941)

In 1920 Robert Engford (1883–1967) of Milwaukee gathered his children into a family acrobatic act that traveled Wisconsin for over twenty years. Born in Germany, as was his son Harry (1905–1973), Engford (originally Engfer) had one of the earliest troupes to tour by truck. The family moved to America in 1911, where Robert and his brother William became active in the *Turnverein*, that source of so many Wisconsin acrobats. William was a contortionist and Robert an acrobat.

Robert and his wife, Amanda (d. 1945), toured for ten months of each year, sometimes using a tent, sometimes appearing in halls. They were the quintessential Wisconsin show, never going outside the state. Though they went as far north as Sturgeon Bay, most of their performances were given in the central part of the state.

Son Harry and daughter Florence were key members of the troupe. Harry was a violinist and accordionist and played winter dates in halls. He had a dance band at one time, taught music, and was active in church choir work. In the summers he and his father's acrobatic duo was the constant in the Engford Family Shows. Others on the roster were George Collins, Charles Riley, George Sterling, and Paul Dukavitch.

The family moved to Plover, Wisconsin, in 1923, where they remained; many of them are buried there. Robert and Harry parted company in 1928, Robert retaining the Engford title and Harry forming Forges' Bros.

Forges' Bros. traveled by truck and railroad, often raising their tent at railroad sidings or in churchyards. Harry made a practice of learning when payday came in the various little towns they visited. They played only matinees, having no generator in the first few years. He married his wife, Lois, in 1936, and she went on tour with him. Forges' Bros. lasted until 1941 and closed because of the war. Robert had closed Engford Family Shows in 1939. After the war, Harry was in vaudeville in the Chicago area with his daughter, Ruthie (b. 1940), who did trapeze and contortion work. In 1964 and 1965, Ruthie (billed as Estrelita) performed with her parents at the Circus World Museum. She married aerialist Frank Clark, and as Francarro and Estrelita they performed an aerial duo, among other acts.

Here the Engford family demonstrates their capability in ground acrobatics and balancing. Mother Lois and father Harry are inverted in bridges, while Harry walks on his hands and Lois forms a hanging cradle. Photograph, undated, Frank and Ruth Engford Clark Gift, Circus World Museum.

THE LINDEMANN BROTHERS (1920–1923)

William (Bill) Lindemann (1882–1949) was inspired to practice acrobatics and rope walking by visiting his father's People's Theatre in Sheboygan, Wisconsin. Circus acts were commonly seen on theatre stages at that time, as part of what we now call variety shows. The young man became proficient enough to be offered a contract by the Thompson Vaudeville Co. of Sandusky, Ohio, in 1903. His brother Gustave (Pete; 1884–1969), who practiced beside Bill, took his first professional job in 1904, with the Cook & Barrett circus. They persevered, though on separate paths for the most part, working for a number of shows until they formed their own circus in 1920.

The brothers' wives were an important part of their careers. Bill married Millie Senkbeil (1890–1966) in December 1904, and they performed as Billy and Millie Lindemann; Pete married Louise Staalson (1889–1968) in 1905, and they toured as Pete and Louise Nelson. In 1914 the two couples combined to form the Lindemann–Nelson act. They were on Ringling Brothers in 1918 and Hagenbeck–Wallace in 1919. Bill and Millie specialized on the Roman rings, Pete and Louise on the trapeze. Of course, they all did ground acrobatics. Albert (Al) Lindemann (1894–1954) was on the 1920 program. He later took up horse and pony training.

The adoption of truck travel by American circuses occurred in the first quarter of the twentieth century. The time of the automobile had come to field shows just as it had to every other aspect of the culture. The "Good Roads" programs, largely promoted by the United States Postal Service (for the benefit of its RFD customers) and by automobile manufacturers (for obvious reasons), led to vast road-building efforts by federal and state authorities. No longer were farm communities isolated by muddy roads in times of bad weather; no longer were freighters limited in the size of their shipments. During the 1920s the road network had advanced to the point where it connected all the population centers in the eastern half of the country.

It was these very places wherein the circus sought its customers. It had reached them in the nineteenth and early twentieth centuries by horse and wagon; later some of them were available by railroad. With the advent of the internal combustion engine, it became possible to service them by automobile, and many, in fact most, of the circuses of the 1930s were truck-borne.

Sam B. Dill, circus owner from Bloomington, Indiana, was one of the first advocates of truck circuses, and he expressed himself in print in *Billboard* in 1931:

> After years of experience with circus organizations of various sizes, both railroad and motorized, I have come to the positive conclusion that the medium-sized show of the future will have to be motorized.

His reasoning was based on considerations of expense, one aspect of which was minimum charges by the railroads that made a ten-mile jump the same price as a forty-mile movement; on flexibility of movement, which was impossible on railroads since the trains could go only where there were tracks; and on maintenance costs, believing that truck travel was easier on both the show equipment and the animals.

Dill expensed a forty-mile movement, comparing his fifty-truck circus to a twenty-five-car railroad circus. Result: It cost $905 to go by rail, $142 to go by truck. Another expert compared the cost of acquisition between a fifty-truck circus and eight railroad cars (sleepers, stock, and flat cars) and reported that the rail equipment (not new) cost twice what a truck show cost.

The earliest motorized circuses used both wagons and trucks. The first show of any size to be wholly truck-borne was Downie Bros.' Circus of 1926, owned by Andrew Downie McPhee. In Wisconsin, the first truck circus was that of the Lindemann brothers.

In 1920, using four Ford trucks, Bill and Pete Lindemann with fourteen people had a successful nineteen-week season. They called the firm Lindemann Bros. and

The circus skills of the four Lindemanns pictured here formed the backbone of their circus operation. They are likely wearing the wardrobe in which they performed. Photograph, undated, Circus World Museum.

Seils–Sterling grew into a famous motorized circus in the 1930s. This is how it looked on the lot shortly after it abandoned its Wisconsin winter quarters. Photograph, 1925, courtesy Sonia Lindemann Barta.

Yankee American Combined Shows. The route they followed in that first season matched those of the wagon-borne shows of previous seasons. They played only the smallest places, avoiding even such small cities as Stevens Point and Fond du Lac. The daily progress, about fourteen miles on average, was the same under either system. However, the truck circus did not have the expense of horses and teamsters. Anyone could drive the trucks. "Doubling in brass," which originally referred to doing an act in the ring and playing an instrument in the band, was expanded to include driving a motor truck. In 1921 the brothers expanded the circus to a nine-truck caravan and had eighteen people with them. In 1922 they had fourteen trucks and twenty-five people. At the end of the 1922 season they wintered in Wisconsin for the last time. Though they maintained their homes in Sheboygan, the circus was located in various states from 1923 to its closing in 1938.

As well as being the earliest of Wisconsin motorized circuses, the Lindemanns were the first to train local people in the circus arts. William Woodcock Sr., the circus historian, once wrote that the Lindemanns were the only circus owners to take farmers and make them into performers. A *Milwaukee Journal* article in 1935 said, "Dozens of young men and women who make up the personnel of the show are Sheboygan products. [The Lindemanns] long since found out that you don't have to go half way around the world to find a daring lad or a graceful young girl who can invent an aerial act or a riding act second to none."

The 1921 title was Lindemann Bros.' World's Greatest Motorized Circus. In the next season the show was called Wm. Seils Wild Animals and Sterling Brothers' Shows Combined. The reason for this has never been made clear. William Seils was William Lindemann, and there were no Sterling brothers. Since Pete Lindemann made no reference to this change in his somewhat voluminous correspondence with historian George Chindahl, the suspicion remains that something was suppressed.

The 1923 show was titled Wm. Seils–Sterling Shows, sometimes shortened to Seils–Sterling, which was managed by Al Lindemann, and it had a brother show titled The Great Danby Show, which was managed by Pete. This was apparently not a successful division, as the Danby chattels were sold at season's end.

No statement has been found to explain why the Seils–Sterling circus wintered in Knoxville, Iowa, in 1923–1924. Problematically, it was much less expensive to rent space at the fairgrounds in Knoxville than to pay to drive twenty-some trucks to Sheboygan. In future years, as the routes spread farther and farther afield, this same rationalization came into play, and the Seils–Sterling Circus was no longer a Wisconsin entity.

E. E. BONHAM (1922–1926)

A pony, a few dogs, and some pigeons were the beginning of the short show business career of Earl E. Bonham (1898–1986) of Prairie du Sac. In 1921 he offered these animals in a carnival sideshow. The next season he organized a small circus, which traveled with a touring car, three trucks, and three horse-drawn wagons.

For advice on how to conduct his enterprise, Bonham went to Evansville, Wisconsin, and consulted the old showman George W. Hall Jr., who not only gave of his vast knowledge, but also agreed to accompany the tiny show. Hall added a trained horse and some ponies to the ensemble but decided after a few weeks that he was too old to travel and withdrew, taking his stock with him. The big show band, which also played in the sideshow, was the next to leave. Bonham struggled on, making a full but not remunerative season. The Holloway brothers (see earlier entry) were on Earl E. Bonham's Trained Animal Show in 1923, which lent a certain professionalism, since most of the show was Bonham and his bears, ponies, and

A number of buildings in downtown Milwaukee have hosted indoor circuses during cold Wisconsin winters. John Agee produced a circus for the Auditorium shortly before he partnered with John Kelley. Photograph, circa 1920, Milwaukee, Wisconsin, Steve Albasing Gift, Circus World Museum.

dogs. After a tour of the north, including Michigan's Upper Peninsula, Bonham put into West Point, Wisconsin, for the winter.

"My favorite territory had always been in the North," he later wrote. "It was a lucky decision to play the towns of Northern Michigan … It was rough, pioneer country, but the money rolled in wherever we showed."

The 1924 circus, of which Bonham was very proud, had more animals, more performers, and even a rope spinner (the wild west contingent). Again his route was through the north country—Wisconsin, Michigan, and Minnesota—and again it was profitable. The 1925 season proved to be similar.

Bonham joined forces for 1926 with a man who owned a carousel. This turned out to be an error, as the machine couldn't easily be moved every day, so they were forced to have weeklong stands. Bonham would take his animals out to theatres and halls in the vicinity, but it was not the same as having a proper circus. They parted at Crystal Falls, Michigan, and Bonham took his portion of the show home. In subsequent years, he exhibited his animals at fairs and on the vaudeville stage, or what passed for it in the small Wisconsin towns. Bonham died in the Veterans Hospital in Middleton, Wisconsin, in 1986.

JOHN M. KELLEY and JOHN AGEE (1924)

To anoint the most bizarre of Wisconsin circuses, it is probably a toss-up between Dr. Morrison's Coliseum (see earlier entry), with its tooth extractions, and "Fun on the Farm," a circus-type exhibition featuring domestic animals. John M. Kelley (1873–1963), former Ringling brothers attorney, and John Agee (1871?–1950), equestrian director of the Ringling circus, formed the latter show in 1924. Agee, a professional horse trainer and rider, had directed a series of winter circuses beginning in 1920. He brought his experience to Kelley's realization of a plan to advertise Wisconsin beef and dairy products by means of an entertainment that utilized bulls, cows, and eighteen of Agee's performing horses. Called by the owners "a combination circus, sideshow and agricultural college," the troupe traveled to various Wisconsin towns and cities in June, July, and August of its only season. It had a green bull (supposedly made so by eating shamrocks), a riding bull, and a clown cow. The show opened in Monroe, Wisconsin, on June 9 and closed at the Wisconsin State Fair in Milwaukee on August 30.

ALVIN MILLER and ELISHA AYERS (1924)

Alvin Miller (1897–1983) was a ceiling walker and ladder balancer on the Lindemann Bros.' circus in 1921 who realized a boyhood dream in 1924 by framing his own circus in Sheboygan, Wisconsin. His effort was financed by his uncle,

John Agee works the crowd while the bull performs one of its tricks in the unusual outdoor ring setup of the Fun on the Farm show. The young men attending the ring were likely Badger farm boys. Photograph, John M. Kelley Gift, Circus World Museum.

The entire cast of the Miller & Ayers show is posed inside the big top. Alvin Miller is to the right of the center pole and his wife, Helen, is on his right. Photograph, 1924, LeRoy Miller Gift, Circus World Museum.

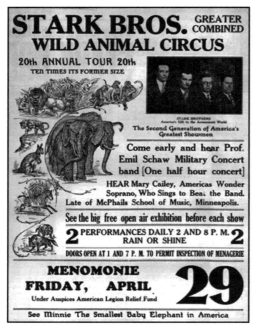

STARK BROS. GREATER COMBINED
WILD ANIMAL CIRCUS
20th ANNUAL TOUR 20th
TEN TIMES ITS FORMER SIZE

STARK BROTHERS
America's Gift to the Amusement World
The Second Generation of America's
Greatest Showmen

Come early and hear Prof.
Emil Schaw Military Concert
band [One half hour concert]

HEAR Mary Cailey, Americas Wonder
Soprano, Who Sings to Beat the Band.
Late of McPhails School of Music, Minneapolis.

See the big free open air exhibition before each show

2 PERFORMANCES DAILY 2 AND 8 P. M. 2
RAIN OR SHINE

DOORS OPEN AT 1 AND 7 P. M. TO PERMIT INSPECTION OF MENAGERIE

MENOMONIE
FRIDAY, APRIL
Under Auspices American Legion Relief Fund
29

See Minnie The Smallest Baby Elephant in America

*There were no Stark brothers, but
Eli Nelson and Walter Picotte may be
included among the four men pictured on
the show's courier. The public affinity for
brother-titled circuses was so great that
a number of showmen fabricated siblings
in this manner. Courier, 1927,
Circus World Museum.*

Elisha Ayers. They used five trucks to carry the big top, a cookhouse, two ponies, and five dogs. Personnel consisted of twelve people who shared performing, setting up, cooking, and truck driving. They limited their route to small towns in Wisconsin and traveled but the one season. In 1925 Miller and his wife, Helen, joined the DeKreko Bros.' Shows of Chicago, a carnival, throwing in the Miller & Ayers' equipment. They were with LaMont Bros.' two-ring motorized circus in 1926 and 1927, and then retired from the business.

ELI NELSON and WALTER PICOTTE (1927–1928)

Eli Nelson, of Fremont, Nebraska, and Walter Picotte organized Stark Brothers Circus in Chippewa Falls, Wisconsin, in 1927. They mounted the show on forty-eight trucks and three buses. Charles Russell Hall, grandson of "Popcorn George" Hall, was the best-known participant, having his Barnyard Circus attached to Stark Bros. Their advertising said 1927 was their twentieth annual tour, but there is no evidence that it was anything but the first. They performed in three rings originally, but by July dwindling crowds forced them to cut the size of the show down to one ring.

There are no references to the Stark Bros. in the 1928 show news until January 1929, when *Billboard* said they had gone on the northern route to California and had a successful season. No more was heard of them.

WILLIAM G. SCHULTZ (1927–1956)

Performing under the pseudonym of Billy Lester, William G. Schultz (1880–1958) of Manitowoc, Wisconsin, had a long career as a circus acrobat. He was proficient at tumbling, trapeze work, teeterboard, and comedy acrobatics. He first appeared in public in 1899 and retired in 1939. The best-known of his affiliations were the Whitney Family Shows, the John Robinson Circus, and Ringling Brothers. However, his real contribution to the circus arts came with his establishment of a circus acrobatic school at the Manitowoc Vocational School in 1927. From this program graduated many circus acrobats who were signed to contracts by all the leading circuses in the country. Schultz's Indoor Circus at the school, produced every other year, was the subject of many magazine and newspaper articles, movie scenes, and television programs. It was, as far as can be determined, the only acrobatic school program in the country. So appreciative of his efforts was the State Board of Vocational and Adult Education of Schultz's work with the young people that he was accredited as a teacher without having earned a college degree. Schultz retired from teaching in 1956 and moved to Bay City, Michigan.

WILLIAM A. GRIFFITH (1957–1965)

It was a nineteenth-century convention that small boys ran away from home to join the circus. "Bill" Griffith (b. 1929) was a grown man who essentially did the same thing. As the owner of a printing business in Appleton, Wisconsin, Griffith was an active member of the community who involved himself in civic functions. One of these involvements was with a circus in 1952, when the local Jaycees sponsored Ringling Brothers and Barnum & Bailey's visit to Appleton. As he worked on the project, he became interested in the people and caught up in the seemingly fascinating world of field shows. He became a circus fan and began attending performances, traveling to other cities to see circuses, and he found a coterie of friends in the circus business. Somewhere along the line he decided to have his own show.

Dolores and Bill Griffith proudly flank their newest acquisition, Bertha, inside the Adams Bros. Circus winter quarters. Photograph, 1958, Appleton, Wisconsin, courtesy Bill Griffith.

Griffith began with an indoor show. Called the Holiday Circus Review, it had an hour-long program of conventional acts. It was out for six weeks in November and December 1957. Jim Lackore has quoted Griffith as saying of this first effort, "Business wasn't great, but it was good. It wasn't so much the financial aspect of it at that point, it was just so heady … it was our circus." To that point the circus had run away with Griffith instead of the reverse.

For 1958 the Griffiths—his wife Dolores was an important part of his show business career—framed a traveling company, Adams Bros. Circus (Griffith's middle name), playing baseball parks and indoor dates. It had a full program, including an elephant act, and was carried on six, later eight, trucks. Again, the finances ended up in the black, but barely. If they had not closed six weeks early, it might have been otherwise. This was the first Wisconsin-based circus to operate since 1941.

The title was changed to Adams Bros. and Seils Bros.' World Toured Shows for 1959. We mentioned Seils Bros. in our remarks on the Lindemanns. With four additional trucks and a new big top, the show left Mexico, Missouri, where it was framed, and moved to the St. Louis area, and then to Chicago. By playing the so-called "Chicago lots," Griffith put the finances into good shape, good enough to have what he later called "a good year—all the way around." If just having his own circus was a heady experience, as it was in 1957, having a full-sized, successful show, such as in 1959, must have been exhilarating.

The Griffith shows operated openly and honestly; there was no grift or gambling. The advertising spoke of it as "America's cleanest show." This was a serious business effort on

Griffith's part; he was trying to make the circus a profitable venture, and he was conscious of the necessity to keep a good name if for no other reason than to protect future profits. As with any showman, he wanted to come back next year.

Two aspects of the business that were manifest by the time Griffith got into it that the old-timers had not had to deal with were sponsorship and telephone solicitation. By selling the program to various civic groups, such as Lions clubs, Kiwanis, American Legion, and Jaycees, the small traveling circuses of the 1930s and subsequent decades were able to have a kind of guarantee of successful appearances. The sponsors did such things as distributing advertising, securing lots and licenses, and, most important, selling tickets in advance of the arrival of the circus.

Telephone solicitation, known as "phone rooms" or "phone banks," is now a common way to sell tickets to anything, whether circus, carnival, theatre events, or even common stocks. The essential idea is to telephone local parties and ask them to purchase circus tickets. Had this system been available to "Popcorn George" Hall, he would no doubt have embraced it.

Of these two methods, often used in combination, sponsorship is by far the most popular with showmen, as it entails no payroll expense for those activities the sponsor agrees to undertake. There are many shows that will visit a town only if sponsorship is available.

Bill Griffith's successful 1959 tour made him enthusiastic about the 1960 season, but his optimism was misplaced. The show was larger, with a menagerie for the first time, and the planned route was the same. The title was now Adams and Sells Circus. They went to the St. Louis area and then played the Chicago lots. But "everything that was right in 1959 was wrong in 1960," Griffith was quoted as saying. Bad weather, inefficient sponsors, and the impounding of the menagerie by the Humane Society ended the season in mid-August in Wisconsin. All but the elephant went to creditors. With the show's demise there was no Wisconsin circus still operating.

The disappointing 1960 season did not dampen the Griffiths' appetite for circus proprietorship. They sat out 1961 and came back in 1962 with a new show, Sells Bros.' 3 Ring Circus. This was a partnership with Robert "Little Bob" Stevens and was a most successful gambit. Traveling on eight trucks and a bus-sleeper, the owners routed the little show from Texas up into Wisconsin and back to Texas. The program was a strong one with a wide variety of acts, and on that basis it deserved the prosperity it achieved. Griffith also credited Stevens with much of the success, because of his ability to "squeeze every penny until it yelled."

Again, a financially excellent season was followed by a less fortunate one. The 1963 version of Sells Bros. played a full season, and the physical assets were impressive, but there grew the making of a schism between the partners, the details of which are not known. Bill Griffith was fully into circus ownership and believed that profits should be maximized. Bob Stevens, for all his penny squeezing, was much in favor of having animal acts and menagerie exhibits. To Griffith, lots of animals meant lots of feed to be bought. At season's end the two men split up the property.

The Griffiths lived in Appleton, but the circus lived in San Antonio, Texas. Birnam Bros. was the title ("so like Barnum," Griffith said) in 1964 when it traveled nearly the same route as had Sells Bros. the year before. By 1965 the show was one that Griffith was proud to own. It had grown in several ways—in wardrobe, in vehicles, and in appearance on the lot—and he was quoted as saying, "I was the proudest of that show—it was the product of eight years of learning."

Having no need to perpetuate the circus aspect of their lives, and wishing to put down roots for the sake of their three daughters, the Griffiths leased the equipment to other parties and joined the ranks of "towners." They had joined out as if fulfilling a private need by becoming public showmen.

WILBUR W. DEPPE (1961–1967)

Growing up in Baraboo, Wisconsin, in a house next to the winter quarters of the Gollmar brothers' circus, and occasionally visiting the Moeller brothers' wagon works on Third Avenue, where many circus wagons were built, wasn't enough to turn Wilbur W. Deppe (1908–1987) into a circus fan. It wasn't until the Circus World Museum was established next to his lumberyard on Water Street in 1959 that, by a kind of osmosis through the fence, he came to appreciate the sawdust realm.

As owner of an assortment of heavy equipment, Deppe was called on by the Museum staff from time to time to do heavy lifting or hauling, and he came to realize what an attraction there was right next door. One of the leaders in the civic life of Baraboo, he became one of the Museum's best friends.

Founded by John M. Kelley, onetime Ringling brothers lawyer, the Museum was initially intended to be just that, a static collection of artifacts. However, C. P. Fox, the second director of the facility, felt the need for a live circus performance on the grounds. Fox was a close friend of Deppe's, and when the latter heard of the need, he bought an elephant from William Griffith of Appleton and lent it to the Museum.

Deppe followed up by buying other animals— ponies, goats, llamas, and more elephants—all of which were used to give a live performance every day the facility was open. To allow the animals to earn their keep in the off-season, Deppe's Classic Country Circus was organized, and with trainers from the Museum it began to travel in the winters. Using two trucks and a trailer, trainer Jenda Smaha, and later John Herriott, took the little show to various venues throughout the eastern half of

John Herriott's liberty pony act always pleased the crowds under the Moeller Hippodrome at Circus World Museum. Here a dozen ponies respond to his commands with a double cartwheel maneuver. Photograph, circa 1964, Circus World Museum.

the country. The show once played in Puerto Rico for six weeks and made a Canadian tour one winter. Department stores and local arenas were often the performance sites.

At its largest the circus had three elephants, a dozen ponies, four dogs, and a chimpanzee. The highlight of its existence was probably the appearance of Smaha and one of the elephants on the Ed Sullivan television show. After six years of proprietorship, Deppe sold the Classic Country Circus to the Circus World Museum. Successor shows have been presented on a daily basis on the Museum grounds since that time.

MURRAY HILL (1971)

After twenty-two years as a musician, nightclub entertainer, and animal trainer, Murray Hill (Murray Seidon) formed his Hill's Great London Circus in 1971. His intent was to play fairgrounds, ballparks, and other outdoor venues in open-air presentations. He had three small elephants ("the world's most untalented elephant act") that he had performed with since 1965. Ron Kelroy's trampoline act (see later entry) was with him, and for the debut show, at Elkhorn, Wisconsin, Hill had Merle Evans as bandleader. Nineteen acts greeted the public at the opening, but Hill reduced this number when he went on tour. Operating out of Burlington, Wisconsin, it was Hill's intent to play towns of populations between 1,000 and 3,000. The circus was on the road just the one season.

Murray Hill acquired his first animal, a chimpanzee in 1955, and later developed an elephant act that grew into a full-fledged circus. Photograph, 1971, Circus World Museum.

WAYNE FRANZEN (1974–1997)

Wisconsin had been without a native traveling circus for three years when a high school teacher in Stevens Point, Wisconsin, opened a show in Rosholt, Wisconsin, on June 14, 1974. Wayne Franzen (1947–1997) had been intent on having a circus career before he was ten years old. Living on a farm, he trained a calf to bow, taught himself to walk the tightrope, and presented shows to neighborhood children. Honoring his father's wishes, he went to school, attended the University, and taught school for six years before he did what he always wanted to do—have his own show. Titled Franzen Brothers Circus, it was owned by Wayne and his brother Neil. They played sixty-eight towns in ninety days in 1974, not an auspicious beginning, as a rule of thumb says a circus should play at least eighty-four of ninety days. Of course, ninety out of ninety is the goal. With as few as nine and as many as twenty-two people on the roster, the one-ring show survived its first season on a program of amateur acrobats and Wayne Franzen's remarkable ability to train animals. He presented goats, dogs, a horse, and an elephant. In time he added a camel and lions and tigers.

The show was based in Amherst Junction, Wisconsin. Neil Franzen dropped out after the first year, but Wayne persevered. Each season he added acts and equipment. Franzen played the smallest of towns, some with as few as 500 people, and he was able to capitalize on the appeal of his animals. As a one-ring circus with a small staff (his mother handled concessions; his sister-in-law was the aerialist), he came to the crossroads villages with a mixture of honest dealings and "down-home" friendliness. Many of the places Franzen visited had never had a live performance other than high school plays. Some of them had no high school.

There were nine acts in the first season; by 1979 there were twenty. The five trucks with which they began business grew to ten. Franzen claimed that he was "out of the red" by 1980, meaning he owned the show free and clear. Unfortunately, "free and clear" in the circus business has meaning only on the day it is expressed. At any moment there may arise a catastrophe to put it all at risk. The outdoor-entertainment business faces the highways, the weather, and the local ordinances as well as the problems inherent in dealing with machinery and animals. And, of course, there is always the specter of bad business. Franzen once said, "You're always in danger of folding … all we need is two weeks with bad crowds."

Visiting 250 towns and villages in a season, and advertising the circus as "America's Favorite Show," Franzen was able to keep his dream alive longer than most small showmen, as we've demonstrated in these pages. For twenty-four years he advanced the cause of nostalgia with a one-ring, small-town show. On a performance basis, Franzen Bros. was a unique circus. Perhaps there had never been one of its size with so many animal acts.

It was one of these acts that ended Wayne Franzen's life. On May 7, 1997, in Carrollton, Pennsylvania, one of his tigers attacked and killed him. He was fifty years old.

Wayne Franzen's great appreciation of animals was readily apparent when he was in the ring or arena with them. Photograph, 1996, by John Preble, courtesy Bernie Bolstad.

RONALD J. KELROY (1979–1997)

Ron Kelroy graduated from his trampoline act to producing circuses for a variety of venues. He often furnished the circus acts for Milwaukee's famous Summerfest. Photograph, undated, John H. McConnell Gift, Circus World Museum.

An Australian by birth, Ronald Kelroy (1940?–1998) emigrated to America with his father, a circus performer who died in this country. Ron then began a career as a freelance performer specializing in trampoline work. He later was in the employ of L. N. Fleckles, well-known producer of Shrine circuses. Kelroy became the director of Fleckles productions and in 1979 went on his own, establishing his headquarters in Trevor, Wisconsin. A competent manager, Kelroy operated under several titles, Royal Australian Circus being the most common usage. Others by which he traveled were Continental Circus, Festival Circus, and Circus Valentine. In some seasons all of these titles were on the road at the same time in various venues, mostly indoor, arena-type presentations under local sponsorship. Kelroy died of cancer in May 1998.

EPILOGUE

The initial affinity between the circus and the State of Wisconsin was geographic. Edmund Mabie found good grazing, plentiful water, and nine-dollar-an-acre land near Delavan. From it he could ply the western roads to Illinois, Iowa, and Missouri months before the eastern shows would arrive.

He found there a place of verdant beauty. As Matthew Buckley wrote, "We are on the very pitch of a perfect prairie where everything flourishes." He said that even the weather far exceeded that in St. Louis, where they had previously wintered. We noted that W. C. Coup said of Delavan that it was "the prettiest place on earth," and that he was so proud of it that he drove P. T. Barnum out to see it.

Once established in Delavan, the Mabie circus drew people to the village who wanted to work for the company. Thus was created a colony composed of performers and workmen whose talents and lifestyles attracted even some of the villagers, and induced them to participate in circus life. In time, other circus troupes were formed, and the lure of the place to professionals became even greater. The Buckleys and the Hollands and their progeny began this trend by moving to Delavan and buying farms, setting a pattern for others. First attracted by the opportunity for employment, many stayed to enjoy and celebrate the land.

In no other place in America did the institution of the circus flower as it did in mid-nineteenth-century Wisconsin. It was as if these participants in an itinerant, rough-and-tumble life used the state as an off-season refuge.

In the midst of the great expansion of population, agriculture, lumbering, and shipping grew this seedling of popular culture that flourished to the point where the Mabies, Burr Robbins, W. C. Coup, and the Ringlings went out from Wisconsin each spring to the corners of the country. And they took the sons and daughters of Wisconsin with them, as performers, as administrators, as workmen. We spoke of the Lindemann brothers "making performers out of farmers," and our lists of little family shows from tiny Wisconsin villages, right down to Wayne Franzen in the 1980s, is a litany of the attraction to be showmen and of the popularity of the genre.

The numbers were not large, no economic force was applied, no political aspiration was present. The traveling circus of the nineteenth century employed close to fifteen hundred Wisconsinites in each season. Yet the state had more shows than any other place at a time when the circus was the leading popular entertainment and was the only live performance most people ever saw.

The traveling circus is gone from Wisconsin, and those that appear there each summer come from other venues. But the performances, the artifacts, even the shape of the tents and the ring are the same as presented by Wisconsin's pioneer showmen for over a hundred years.

Slices of the circus remain. Each summer the city of Milwaukee hosts a great nostalgic circus street parade, the Great Circus Parade, to which thousands of people come, lining the curbs to see teams of horses pulling restored show wagons, cages of beasts, and brass bands from all over America. At Baraboo, the State Historical Society of Wisconsin owns the Circus World Museum, the largest facility in the world devoted to the preservation of the history of a single type of entertainment enterprise.

NOTES

MABIE BROTHERS—Chapter 1

The preliminary investigation into the history of the Mabie brothers was made by Gordon Yadon of Delavan (*Bannerline*, May 1, 1965). The land transfers to the Mabies are listed in the George L. Chindahl papers at Circus World Museum. William M. Davis Jr. in the *New York Clipper*, January 19, 1892, relates the adoption by Jerry Mabie of the "camp outfit." Peter Conklin, the clown, who was notorious for misdating his reminiscences in various publications, wrote one version of the "pink lemonade" story for *Billboard* of December 16, 1911. Wayne A. Landerholm and Mrs. Daniel R. LaBar kindly made available certain Mabie family documents.

DELAVAN'S CIRCUS COLONY—Chapter 2

Gordon Yadon wrote a series of articles on Delavan circus personalities for *Bannerline* in 1965. The Buckley Hippodrome comments appear in Stuart Thayer and William M. Slout's book, *Grand Entree* (San Bernardino, 1998). David Lano's remarks are from *A Wandering Showman, I* (East Lansing, 1957).

HIRAM ORTON—Chapter 3

Information on Hiram Orton and his family came from Melvern Orton of Alameda, California; from *An Account of Hiram Orton and his Descendants* (Burlington, Iowa, 1900) by Laura F. Marsh Orton; from the E. C. May papers at Circus World Museum; and from George Chindahl, "An Orton Route Book," in *White Tops*, March–April 1956. Correspondence between Mrs. William H. Woodcock (Sadie Orton) and Judge Don Binkowski was also of value. Adrian D. Sharpe wrote "The Orton Circus," a history, which appeared in *Bandwagon* (July–August 1969).

DAN CASTELLO—Chapter 4

Gordon Yadon wrote a biography of Castello in *Bannerline*, March 15, 1968. George Chindahl's papers at Circus World Museum contain much Castello material, but Chindahl never wrote of him. There is an undated lengthy interview with Castello in the *Syracuse* (N.Y.) *Standard* of 1899. His circus career is outlined in *Grand Entree* by Thayer and Slout, mentioned previously.

WILLIAM CAMERON COUP—Chapter 5

The *New York Clipper* article quoted at the beginning of this chapter was written by Kit Clarke and published in 1871. Coup's autobiography, *Sawdust and Spangles*, assembled from notes he left, was organized by Forrest Crissey and published in New York in 1901. Coup himself wrote the story of the founding of the Barnum Circus in the *New York Clipper*, May 16, 1891. The Arthur Saxon biography of Barnum referred to in the text is *P. T. Barnum, the Legend and the Man* (New York, 1989). The history of Coup's 1882 circus is in John Polacsek, "The Demise and Disposition of the 1882 Coup Circus," *Bandwagon*, September–October 1984.

BURR ROBBINS—Chapter 6

Keith McLaughlin, of Janesville, has collected a large amount of information on Robbins, which he shared with us. David W. Watt's articles in the *Janesville Daily Gazette* from 1912 to 1920 delineate his career as Robbins's ticket seller and general factotum. Ted Bowman of Hugo, Oklahoma, provided many of Robbins's routes.

THE HALL FAMILY—Chapter 7

Ruth Ann Montgomery, of Evansville, Wisconsin, wrote the most complete history of the Hall family. It was published in a series in the *Evansville Review* in 1997. George W. Hall was the subject of several long interviews in the press. Among these was one in *Billboard* published June 14, 1902, and one in the *Chicago Sunday Tribune*, April 13, 1913. Orin Copple King's history of the circus in Kansas, which ran for years in *Bandwagon*, beginning in 1987, twice reported on Hall's visits to that state. Walter Jr. and Ruth Gollmar, in interviews by the authors, revealed much information on the Hall family.

THE RINGLING BROTHERS—Chapter 8

Unlike most of the showmen whose professional lives are chronicled here, the Ringling brothers provided a large amount of information on their own careers. Alfred (Alf T.) Ringling wrote *Life Story of the Ringling Brothers* (Chicago, 1900); Charles Ringling left notes that he intended to publish as a book. They now rest in the John and Mable Ringling Museum of Art in Sarasota, Florida. John Ringling was the reputed author of several magazine articles. J. J. Schlicter in *Wisconsin Magazine of History* (volume 26, number 1, 1942) researched the early days of the family. C. P. Fox's *A Ticket to the Circus* is one of the better examinations of the show, especially because of its inclusion of Alice Ringling Coerper's memories of her father and uncles. Perhaps the best book on the Ringlings is Henry Ringling North and Alden Hatch's *The Circus Kings* (New York, 1960). Many ex-employees wrote of their experiences while with the circus, and there were hundreds of articles published in magazines and newspapers across the country. The *New York Clipper* and *Billboard*, in the files of Circus World Museum, were the source of much Ringling material.

THE GOLLMAR BROTHERS—Chapter 9

Robert H. Gollmar's book, *My Father Owned a Circus* (Caldwell, Idaho, 1965), is the only full-length history of Gollmar Bros.' Circus. The Baraboo newspapers, the *Sauk County Democrat* and the *Baraboo Republic*, covered much of the day-to-day operations. Bound copies of each are at Circus World Museum. The ledgers of the circus are also in that depository. Interviews with Walter Jr. and Ruth Gollmar provided insight into the Gollmar family history.

A MULTITUDE OF SHOWS—Chapter 10

Forty-one circuses are chronicled in this chapter, and the information on each of them was provided by a different source. We list here the name of each show owner and the principal source of the information we have documented.

ANDREW HAIGHT and GEORGE DeHAVEN—Dean Jensen, *The Biggest, the Smallest, the Longest, the Shortest* (Madison, Wisconsin, 1975) contains a biography of Andrew Haight.

HERMAN A. FISTLER—The *New York Clipper*, October 5, 1867, is the source of the only reference to this circus.

GREENLEAF W. COLLINS—Gordon Yadon in *Bannerline*, August 1, 1965, offers a two-page outline of Collins's career.

DR. GEORGE MORRISON—Gordon Yadon wrote "Dr. George Morrison, a Memorable Personality," which was published in *White Tops*, January–February 1969.

JOE PARSON and FRANK ROY—Charles Schluter did research in the Darlington Public Library, which the authors used in the preparation of their section on Joe Parson and Frank Roy. Marion Howard of Darlington provided genealogical and historical information about these gentlemen.

THE SKERBECK FAMILY—George Chindahl published a history of the Skerbecks in *White Tops*, July 1955.

EPH WILLIAMS—The *Medford*, Wisconsin, *Star & News* has a biography of Williams in its April 25, 1891, issue. He is mentioned prominently in Chindahl's 1955 article on the Skerbeck family (see preceding entry).

HARRY CASTELLO—Ben Hecht, the playwright and journalist, in his autobiographical *A Child of the Century* (New York, 1954), has a long description of life in the Castello household in Racine.

GIBBONS & CHAPMAN—The *New York Clipper* was the source of our information on this short-lived venture.

CHARLES C. McDONALD—All that we learned of McDonald's career came from notices in the *New York Clipper*.

THE MILLER BROTHERS—The columns of the *Necedah Republican* and the *New York Clipper* provided much material on the Millers. Harlowe Hoyt in *Town Hall Tonight* (Englewood Cliffs, New Jersey, 1955) comments on the Millers. Like them, Hoyt was a native of Beaver Dam.

L. J. RODICUE/RODRIGUEZ—There were several references to Rodicue's circus in the 1889 *New York Clipper*.

THE WINTERMUTE BROTHERS—C. P. Fox wrote a short history of Wintermute Bros.' Circus for *Bandwagon* in its November–December 1959 issue. The Whitewater, Wisconsin, *Sentinel* printed an interview with Zella Wintermute Hall in the 1940s. Isaac Marcks's vast file of routes and rosters at Circus World Museum includes the Wintermute circuses from 1907 to 1938.

THE STANG BROTHERS—Don Hensey of Kenosha, Wisconsin, who has collected material on the Stang brothers for some time, made this available to us. Gordon Yadon did a short treatment in *Bannerline*, December 15, 1968, and George Chindahl researched the brothers in 1954.

THE HOLLOWAY BROTHERS—These brothers were on so many shows that references to them are found both in the public press and in trade journals in the years they were active.

ANTHONY WHITE—Our references to White were all found in the *New York Clipper*.

THE MARSHALL BROTHERS—The principal source for information on the Marshalls is the R. E. Conover files at Beavercreek, Ohio, and a chapter in Jensen's *The Biggest, the Smallest, the Longest, the Shortest* (see under Haight).

WILLIAM J. ASH—Harry Lakola wrote a short piece in the June–July 1936 *White Tops*, and Marian S. Revett mentioned William Ash's career in *A Minstrel Town* (New York, 1955). Those and the *New York Clipper* were our sources.

HERBERT L. MARSHALL—The pages of the *New York Clipper* provided what we learned of H. L. Marshall.

F. W. BURNS—John Hanus of Antigo, Wisconsin, made his father's papers available to us for our research into Burns, Boldt & Hanus. The show was further identified in the *New York Clipper*.

ROBERT V. HALL—The newspapers of Fond du Lac, Wisconsin, and the R. E. Conover files in Beavercreek, Ohio, were the principal sources for information on Hall.

EMIL SEIBEL—Just as the Baraboo newspapers reported every move of the Ringlings and the Gollmars, so the *Watertown Daily Times* covered Emil Seibel and his circus activities. Two men, Gary Buggs of Edgerton, Wisconsin, and Gerald Schubert, of Watertown, recorded all the entries in the paper. Their manuscripts are at the library of Circus World Museum.

GEORGE E. WAGNER—The *New York Clipper* and *Billboard* supplied what we know of Wagner's activities.

CARL M. DALTON—Norman Wilbert and Frank H. Thompson commented on Dalton's activities in chronicling other persons. Bill Petersen provided materials on Dalton from the holdings of the La Crosse Public Library. No researcher has yet seen fit to go into Dalton's career.

DODE FISK—George Chindahl in *White Tops*, January–February 1953, published "Dode Fisk, Playboy and Showman," the best biography thus far written about Fisk. There is a collection of Fisk material at the Wonewoc Public Library.

CORLISS BULGER and DUDLEY CHENEY—Audrey Johnson, Monroe County historian, provided articles from the Sparta newspapers. Rita Resman, Necedah historian, did the same for newspapers in that town.

THE BEVERUNG BROTHERS—The *New York Clipper* and *Billboard* each had references to the Beverung show in 1914.

ALBERT HODGINI—John Daniel Draper, in *Bandwagon*, May–June 1993, covered Albert and all the other family members in his article, "The Riding Hodgini Family." Others who have published comments include Bob Taber, the Hodgini Family (*White Tops*, May–June 1961), and Barry L. Dubuque, "The Original Miss Daisy" (*Bandwagon*, November–December 1979).

H. R. J. MILLER—*Billboard* magazine and the files at Circus World Museum provided the data on Miller's short-lived circus.

THE ENGFORD FAMILY—Ruthie Engford Clark of Chesterton, Indiana, provided a sheaf of notes on the history of her family, which rounded out the material (posters, heralds, newspaper items, and so on) in the Circus World Museum collection. Clark also submitted to an interview on her family's involvement with the circus and other popular entertainment.

THE LINDEMANN BROTHERS—Norman H. Wilbert, in *White Tops*, gave a short history of the Lindemanns in the May–June 1971 issue. The files of the *Sheboygan Press* provided much information. Perhaps the correspondence between "Pete" Lindemann and George Chindahl is the best source of the history of the show. This lies in the Chindahl files at Circus World Museum.

E. E. BONHAM—Earl Bonham published a pamphlet, *One Ring Circus* (n.p., n.d.), that describes his career and his thoughts on operating a small show. *Billboard* was the only other source of Bonham notices.

JOHN M. KELLEY and JOHN AGEE—Articles in the Madison and Baraboo newspapers were the main source of information on Kelley. Agee's name appeared in *Billboard* every season for many years. Both men assembled scrapbooks that are in the files of Circus World Museum.

ALVIN MILLER and ELISHA AYERS—The only published account of the Miller–Ayers Shows is the one by Norman H. Wilbert that appeared in *Bandwagon*, November–December 1972.

ELI NELSON and WALTER PICOTTE—There is a file on Nelson at Circus World Museum that was utilized by the authors.

WILLIAM G. SCHULTZ—"Billy" Schultz's work with youngsters was the subject of many articles in national publications such as *Saturday Evening Post* and *American Magazine*. Television and newsreel coverage was also quite extensive. William G. Schultz, Jr., wrote a short biography of his father that is in the Circus World Museum collection.

WILLIAM A. GRIFFITH—Personal interviews with Griffith were important to this reconstruction of his career. Articles on Griffith by Jim Lackore were in *Bandwagon* in successive issues in 1974. Several reviews of Griffith-owned circuses appeared in *White Tops* over the years.

WILBUR W. DEPPE—Articles in the *Baraboo News–Republic* were our source for the history of Deppe's involvement with the circus.

MURRAY HILL—Various Shrine circus programs and that of Hill's Great London Circus provided us with information on Hill's career.

WAYNE FRANZEN—Small-town newspapers were a good source of Franzen material. A CNN television segment gave wide publicity to the circus.

RONALD J. KELROY—John H. McConnell in *Shrine Circus* (Detroit, 1998) devoted space to Kelroy's involvement with Shrine presentations. There was also newspaper coverage.

In addition to the specific contributions listed here, we must acknowledge the research of George L. Chindahl of Maitland, Florida, and Richard E. Conover of Beavercreek, Ohio. The Chindahl papers rest in the archives at Circus World Museum, while those of Conover are held by his son, Albert Conover.

Previously published work that concerned itself with Wisconsin's circus history includes:

Wisconsin Circus Lore, published by the Federal Writer's Project (Madison, Wisconsin, 1937)

Wisconsin Circus Lore by Dorothy Moulding Brown (n.p., 1947)

The Circus, Wisconsin's Unique Heritage by Richard E. Conover (Circus World Museum, Baraboo, 1967)

The Biggest, the Smallest, the Longest, the Shortest by Dean Jensen (Wisconsin House Book Publishers, Madison, 1975)

The business records of circuses formed in Wisconsin are nearly nonexistent. Similarly, the personal papers of the proprietors have had a low rate of survival. As a result, a work such as this book places a heavy emphasis on the news of circuses printed in the newspapers and periodicals of the time. Their reporting provides one of the few available information continuums about the traveling show industry. Foremost among these are the weekly popular entertainment magazines *New York Clipper*, published in New York (1853–1924), and *Billboard*, out of Cincinnati (1894–1960). "The Old Reliable" and "the Bible of the Outdoor Show Business," as they were respectively nicknamed, provided weekly synopses of circus activity that took place across America.

Staff support and research assistance was provided by Bernice Zimmer and Erin Foley. The grant under which it was possible to produce this volume came from the Wisconsin Sesquicentennial Commission. Additional support was provided by Bill Griffith of Spring Green, Wisconsin. The grant was administered in Baraboo by Karen Severson. Greg Parkinson, Executive Director of the Circus World Museum, extended us the use of the facilities and files at the Museum's Robert L. Parkinson Library and Research Center.

INDEX

Hill, Murray (Seidon), 126

Hiram, Minnie, 53

Hiram, Sally, 53

Hiram, Willie, 53

Hocum, Elbridge, 92

Hodgini, Albert D., 115

Hodgini, Joseph Henry
(Hodges), 115

Holland, Edward, 17, 18,
19, 20, 21

Holland, George E., 19,
20

Holland, George F., 17,
18, 19, 21, 29, 105

Holland, John (Lucien),
13, 16, 17

Holland, John Jr., 17, 18,
19

Holland, Mary Ann, 17,
18

Hollister, Eugene B., 21

Holloway, Art, 108

Holloway, Claude, 108

Holloway, Eddie, 108

Holloway, Frank, 108

Holloway, Katherine, 18,
19

Holloway, Max, 108

Hoonsinger, Herr, 5

Howes, Egbert, 31, 33, 35

Howes, Frank, 61, 66

Howes, Nathan A., 1, 2,
3, 17, 59

Howes, Seth B., 2, 3, 5,
6, 7, 9, 10, 13, 31, 50

Howes, Wilson, 2

Hurd, S. H., 41

Huyk, Isaac, 25

Hyatt, Oscar, 14

Innes, Will A., 103

Jamison, Fannie, 10, 11

Johnson, J. A., 62

Juliar, Mary, 87, 88

Juliar, Salome, 87

Julien, Master, 17

Kelley, John M., 80, 121,
125

Kelroy, Ronald J., 126,
128

Kennedy, R. S., 24, 25

Kent, Jule, 33

Kimball, E. M., 76

King, Orin C., 64, 65

Kipp, Dan, 25

Lackore, Jim, 123

Landers, Ernest, 90

Lano, David, 18

Leaman, Mademoiselle,
10

Lee Family, 52

Lent, Lewis B., 32

Leon, Madame, 52

Lillie, Gordon (Pawnee
Bill), 75, 85

Lindemann, Albert (Al),
117, 120

Lindemann, Gustave
(Pete Nelson), 117,
118, 119, 120

Lindemann, Louise
(Staalson, Nelson),
117

Lindemann, Millie
(Senkbeil), 117

Lindemann, William
(Bill, Seils), 113, 117,
118, 119

Lipman, Mike, 17

Litt, Jacob, 103

Longbotham, Frank, 68

Loretta Twins, 114

Lowanda Family, 33

Lowanda, Abelardo, 33

Lowanda, Alexander, 33

Lowanda, Martinho, 33

Lowanda, Natilio, 33

Mabie, Edmund, 1, 2, 3,
5, 6, 10, 11, 12, 13,
14, 17, 129

Mabie, Elizabeth Gifford,
1

Mabie, Jeremiah, 1, 2, 3,
6, 8, 9, 11, 12, 13

Mabie, Joshua, 1

Macart, Frank, 65, 66,
67, 91

Macart, Fred, 68

Macart, Vivian, 68

Macarte, Marie, 66

Madden, George, 18, 37,
41, 96

Madden, Mary Ann, 18,
41

Madden, Nora, 18

Main, Walter L., 20

Marginley, B. R., 17

Marks, Hiram, 53

Marshall, Charles, 109

Marshall, Edward, 109

Marshall, Herbert L., 109

Marshall, Matthew, 109